Principles of Lending

Nirmala Lee

GLOBAL
professional
publishing

This edition published by Global Professional Publishing 2008

Global Professional Publishing

European Innovation Centre, Fitzroy House

11 Chenies Street

London WC1E 7EY

United Kingdom

Email: publishing@gppbooks.com

ISBN: 978-1-906403-20-1

Printed in the United States by Integrated Book Technology

Author Information

Nirmala Lee is Senior Lecturer in Banking at London Metropolitan University Business School. Her 37-year career in banking and banking education has encompassed senior management positions in State Bank of India for 25 years as well as consultancy with Barclays Premier International. She is a member of the industry regulator FSA and NIACE Advisory Group on Financial Literacy for Older People, as well as the Financial Education Qualification Accreditation Group. She has served on the steering group of the Financial Services Skills Council (FSSC), and on the directorate of the Teachers and Trainers of Financial Services (TTFS). She is a Fellow of the Chartered Institute of Bankers (FCIB) as well as a Fellow of the Higher Education Academy (FHEA). Her paper on risks in investing in emerging markets was circulated at the World Bank/IMF Conferences at Hong Kong, and she co-authored a report on 'Financial Literacy Education and Skills Life' on behalf of the National Research and Development Centre for literacy and numeracy (NRDC) for the DfES. She is pursuing research in financial literacy at the Institute of Education, University of London.

Acknowledgements

ifs *School of Finance* would like to thank Stewart Fryer and Derek Lucas for their contributions in the preparation of this text.

Contents

References

Arora, A. (1997) *Practical Banking and Building Society Law*, Blackstone Press, London.

Barth, J. R., Caprio, G. and Levine, R. (2007) *Rethinking Bank Regulation: Till Angels Govern*, Cambridge University Press, Cambridge.

Basel (2000) *Principles for the Management of Credit Risk*, Basel Committee on Banking Supervision, Basel.

Basel, B. C. o. B. S. (2006) *Basel II: International Convergence of Capital Measurement and Capital Standards: A Revised Framework – Comprehensive Version*, Bank for International Settlements, Basel.

Berger, A. N. and Udell, G. F. (2004) 'The institutional memory hypothesis and the procyclicality of bank lending behavior', *Journal of Financial Intermediation*, **13**, 458-495.

Bessis, J. (2002) *Risk Management in Banking*, John Wiley and Sons Ltd, Chichester.

Bharath, S., Dahiya, S., Saunders, A. and Srinivasand, A. (2007) 'So what do I get? The bank's view of lending relationships', *Journal of Financial Economics*, **85**, 368-419.

Buttonwood (2007) In *The Economist*.

Carletti, E., Cerasi, V. and Daltung, S. (2007) 'Multiple-bank lending: Diversification and free-riding in monitoring', *Journal of Financial Intermediation*, **16**, 425-451.

Chakraborty, S. and Ray, T. (2006) 'The development and structure of financial systems', *Journal of Economic Dynamics and Control*.

Chant, J. F. (1970) 'Security, Default Allowances, and Risk Preference', *The Quarterly Journal of Economics*, **84**, 688-695.

CitizensAdvice (2003) *Evaluation Report*, Citizens Advice, pp. Ev 234-235.

Cotis, J.-P. (2007) *OECD Sees Sharp U.S. Economic Slowdown* 9.5.2007.

Crook, J. N., Edelman, D. B. and Thomasc, L. C. (2007) 'Recent developments in consumer credit risk assessment', *European Journal of Operational Research*, **183**, 1447-1465.

Cruickshank, D. (2000) *Competition in UK Banking: A Report to the Chancellor of the Exchequer*.

DeAngelo, H., DeAngelo, L. and Wruck, K. H. (2002) 'Asset liquidity, debt covenants, and managerial discretion in financial distress: the collapse of L.A. Gear', *Journal of Financial Economics*, **64**, 3-34.

Devenow, A. and Welch, I. (1996) 'Rational herding in financial economics', *European Economic Review*, **40**, 603-615.

DTI (2003a) *Second Report of the Task Force on Tackling Over-indebtedness*, DTI Task Force on Tackling Over-indebtedness, London, pp. pg 12.

DTI (2003b) *Sustainability and Business Competitiveness*, Department of Trade and Industry in association with Forum for the Future, London.

Ellison, A., Collard, S. and Forster, R. (2006) *Illegal lending in the UK*, DTI, London.

Ellithorn, C. (2007) In *The Times*, London, pp. 57.

FOS (2003) 'Credit cards – equal liability under section 75 of the Consumer Credit Act 1974', *Ombudsman News*, **31**.

FSA (2003) *Mortgage Regulation*, Financial Services Authority, London.

FSA (2006a) London. FSA (2006b) *Risk Management*.

FSA (2007a) Financial Services Authority.

FSA (2007b) *Treating customers fairly – culture*, Financial Services Authority, London.

Gonzalez, L. and James, C. (2007) 'Banks and bubbles: How good are bankers at spotting winners?' *Journal of Financial Economics*, **86**, 40-70.

Greenspan, A. (2001) In *Chicago Bank Structure Conference, May 10, 2001*, Chicago.

Hall, G. and Young, B. (1991) 'Factors Associated with Insolvency amongst Small Firms', *International Small Business Journal*, **9**, 54-63.

Heaney, V. (2007) 'A repackaged crisis', *Financial World*, 14-16.

Heffernan, S. A. (2002) 'How do UK financial institutions really price their products?' *Journal of Banking & Finance*, **26**, 1997–2016.

Hempel, G. H. and Simonson, D. G. (1999) *Bank Management*, John Wiley & Sons Inc., Chichester.

Hyytinen, A. and Toivanen, O. (2004) 'Monitoring and market power in credit markets', *International Journal of Industrial Organization*, **22**, 269-288.

Kapoor, J., Dlabay, L. and Hughes, R. (2004) *Personal Finance*, McGraw Hill Irwin, London.

Levitt, A. (2007) 'Conflicts and the Credit Crunch', *The Wall Street Journal*.

Marriott, P., Edwards, J. R. and Mellett, H. (2002) *Introduction to Accounting*, Sage Publications, London.

Mason, J. R. (2007) 'Mortgage Loan Modification: Promises and Pitfalls', *Criterion Economics*.

Mateut, S., Bougheas, S. and Mizen, P. (2006) 'Trade credit, bank lending and monetary policy transmission', *European Economic Review*, **50**, 603-629.

Matthews, K., Murinde, V. and Zhaoc, T. (2007) 'Competitive conditions among the major British banks', *Journal of Banking & Finance*, **31**, 2025-2042.

Matthews, K. and Thompson, J. (2005) *The Economics of Banking*, John Wiley and Sons Ltd, Chichester.

Micco, A. and Panizza, U. (2006) 'Bank ownership and lending behavior', *Economics Letters*, **93**, 248-254.

Pike, R. and Neale, B. (2006) *Corporate Finance and Investment*, Prentice Hall Financial Times, London.

Pilbeam, K. (2005) *Finance and Financial Markets*, Palgrave Macmillan, London.

Porter, M. E. (1980) *Competitive Strategy*, Free Press.

Raquel Florez-Lopeza (2007) 'Modelling of insurers' rating determinants. An application of machine learning techniques and statistical models', *European Journal of Operational Research*, **183**, 1488-1512.

Riding, A. L. and Haines, G. (2001) 'Loan guarantees Costs of default and benefits to small firms', *Journal of Business Venturing*, **16**, 595-512.

Röthelia, T. F. (2001) 'Competition, herd behavior, and credit cycles: evidence from major Swiss Banks', *Journal of Economics and Business*, **53**, 585-592.

Ruhnka, J. C. and Young, J. E. (1987) 'A venture capital model of the development process for new ventures', *Journal of Business Venturing*, **2**, 167-184.

Ruhnka, J. C. and Young, J. E. (1991) 'Some hypotheses about risk in venture capital investing', *Journal of Business Venturing*, **6**, 115-133.

Saunders, A. and Cornett, M. M. (2006) *Financial Institutions Management: A Risk Management Approach*, McGraw-Hill, London.

Saxby, S. (2006) 'Court of Appeal increases UK consumer protection for overseas credit purchases', *Computer Law & Security Report*, **22**, 181-182.

Smith, T. (1996) *Accounting for Growth*, Random House, London.

Taylor, M. (2007) 'Basel travel bag', *Financial World*, July/August 2007, 22-24.

Touhey, K. (1997) In *Chartered Banker*, Vol. January 1997.

Treasury (2003) *The Transparency of Credit Card Charges*, House of Commons, Session 2003-04, Select Committee on Treasury – First Report, London.

Wernick, A. S. (1991) 'How to perfect security interest in software', *Computer Law & Security Report*, **7**, 61-62.

Willingham, J. (1997) *International Handbook of Corporate Finance*, Glenlake Publishing Company Ltd./Fitzroy Dearborn Publishers, London.

Wilson Committee (1979) *The Financing of Small Firms, Interim Report of the Committee to Review the Functioning of the Financial Institutions*, HMSO, London.

Yang, B., Lib, L. X. and Xu, H. J. J. (2001) 'An early warning system for loan risk assessment using artificial neural networks', *Knowledge-Based Systems*, **14**, 303-306.

Abbreviations

ABI	The Association of British Insurers
ABL	Asset-based lending
ABS	Asset-backed securities
AER	Annual equivalent rate
ANN	Artificial neural networks
APR	Annual percentage rate
AST	Assured shorthold tenancy
BBA	British Bankers' Association
BCC	British Chambers of Commerce
BERR	Department for Business, Enterprise and Regulatory Reform
BSA	Basic Skills Agency; Building Societies Association
CA	Citizens' Advice
CILA	Certificate of Independent Legal Advice
CRM	Credit risk mitigation
CVA	Company voluntary arrangement
CVL	Creditors' voluntary liquidation
DTI	Department for Trade and Industry
FICO	Fair Isaac Credit Organization (or Fair Isaac and Company)
FLA	Finance and Leasing Association
FOS	Financial Ombudsman Service
FRS	Financial Reporting Standard
FSA	Financial Services Authority
HLR	Higher lending charge
HMT	Her Majesty's Treasury

IAS	International accounting standard
IFA	Independent financial adviser
ISDA	International Swaps and Derivatives Association
LMA	Loan Market Association
LTV	Loan to value
M&A	Mergers and acquisitions
MBS	Mortgage-backed securities
MIG	Mortgage indemnity guarantee
OFT	Office of Fair Trading
RAROC	Risk adjusted return on capital
ROT	Retention of title
S&P	Standard and Poor
SFLG	Small Firms Loan Guarantee
SME	Small- and medium-sized enterprise
SSAP	Statement of Standard Accounting Practice
SVR	Standard variable rate
VAR	Value at risk

List of statutes

Bank of England Act 1998

Charities Act 1992, 1993, 2006

Civil Liberty (Contribution) Act (1978)

Companies Act 2006

Company Directors Disqualification Act 1986

Consumer Credit Act 1974, 2006

Data Protection Act 1998

Enterprise Act 2002

Family Law Reform Act 1969

Financial Services and Markets Act 2000

Freedom of Information Act 2000

Infants Relief Act 1874

Insolvency Act 1986, 1994, 2000

Insurance Companies Act 1980

Land Registration Act, 2002

Law of Property (Miscellaneous Provisions) Act 1989

Law of Property Act, 1925, 1969

Life Assurance Act, 1774

Limitation Act 1980

Limited Liability Partnership Act 2000

Limited Partnerships Act 1907

Minors' Contracts Act 1987

Partnership Act 1890

Policies of Assurance Act 1867

Statute of Frauds 1677

Trustee Act 1925, 2000

Trusts of Land and Appointment of Trustees Act 1996

Unfair Contract Terms Act 1977

List of cases

Allcard v Skinner [1887]

Aluminium Industrie Vaassen BV v Romalpa Aluminium Ltd [1976]

Avon Finance Co Ltd v Bridger [1985]

Bache & Co (London) Ltd v Banque Vernes et Commercials De Paris SA [1973]

Bank of Baroda v Panessar [1987]

Bank of Montreal v Sperling Hotel Co Ltd [1973]

Barclays Bank plc v Boulter and Boulter [1999]

Barclays Bank plc v O'Brien [1994]

Bigger staff v Rowatt's Wharf Ltd [1896]

Bradford Old Bank Ltd v Sutcliffe [1918]

Brandao v Barnett [1846]

Buckingham and Co v London and Midland Bank [1895]

Church of England Building Society v Piskor [1954]

Coutts v Browne-Lecky [1947]

Cuthbert v Robarts Lubbock and Co [1909]

Davies v Humphreys [1840]

Dearle and Hall [1828]

Devaynes v Noble, Clayton's Case [1816]

Deverges v Sandeman Clark & Co [1902]

Dobbs v National Bank of Australasia Ltd [1935]

Evans v Rival Granite Quarries Ltd [1910]

Foster v McKinnon [1869]

Garnett v M'Kewan [1872]

Harrold v Plenty [1909]

Joachimson v Swiss Bank Corpn [1921]

Kelner v Baxter [1866]

Lindenau v Desborough [1828]

Lloyds Bank Ltd v Bundy [1975]

London Assurance v Mansel [1879]

Moschi v LEP Air Services Ltd [1973]

Myers v United Guarantee and Life Assurance Co [1855]

National Provincial Bank of England v Brackenbury [1906]

National Provincial Bank of England v Glanusk [1913]

National Westminster Bank plc v Morgan [1985]

National Westminster Bank plc v Spectrum Plus Ltd [2005]

Nottingham Permanent Benefit Building Society v Thurstan [1903]

Office of Fair Trading v Lloyds Bank plc, Tesco Personal Finance Ltd, and American Express Services Europe Ltd [2006]

Orakpo v Manson Investments Ltd [1978]

Provincial Bank of Ireland v Donnell [1934]

RA Cripps and Son Ltd v Wickenden [1973]

R v Wilson [1879] *Re Browne's Policy* [1903]

Re Brumark Investments Ltd [2001] (New Zealand)

Re Marketing Consortium Ltd [1989]

Re Panama, New Zealand and Australian Royal Mail Co [1870]

Re William C Leitch Brothers Ltd [1933]

Re Yorkshire Woolcombers Association [1903]

Robin v Smith [1985]

Rouse v Bradford Banking Co [1894]

Royal Bank of Scotland plc v Etridge [2001]

Royal Bank of Scotland v Christie [1841]

Salomon v Salomon and Co Ltd [1897]

Sheffield Corporation v Barclay [1905]

Siebe Gorman & Co Ltd v Barclays Bank Ltd [1979]

Titford Property v Cannon Street Acceptances Ltd [1975]

United Bank of Kuwait v Sahib [1996]

Ward v National Bank of New Zealand [1883]

West Bromwich Building Society v Wilkinson [2005]

Whittington v Whittington – National Westminster Intervening [1978]

Williams and Glyn's bank Ltd v Barnes [1980]

Williams and Glyn's Bank Ltd v Boland [1980]

Yourell v Hibernian Bank Ltd [1918]

Preface

This text has been specifically written for students taking the *Principles of Lending* (PRIL) module of the **ifs** *School of Finance* Applied Diploma in Financial Services Management. It is also intended to serve as a reference text for all students of lending.

The scope of the text

Lending money is a core skill within the financial services industry. As such, it is crucial that customers have a quality experience and this can only be provided by staff with an understanding of the subject. Customers expect lenders to have a full and detailed knowledge of the legal and compliance aspect of their roles; these expectations include relevant case and statute law along with the more recent developments in the Banking Code and Business Banking Code, plus the implications of initiatives such as Treating Customers Fairly and Responsible Lending.

Lenders need to be aware of the diversity of customers that could approach them for the wide range of lending services provided in today's financial markets. A lack of understanding of the nature of the customer, or the details of the lending request can result in the lender recommending the wrong product to the customer, or not being able to recover an advance because the lender was not aware of the legal implications of lending to that particular customer type.

The nature of lending does mean that occasionally the lender will not be able to recover the whole debt from the customer. It is through an appreciation of the risks involved in lending, and an ability to reduce those risks, that providers are able to make better decisions. A full understanding of the lending cycle undoubtedly reduces the risks. The lending cycle starts with the lending decision (including an analysis of financial information), and includes monitoring and control plus the ability to detect early warning signals, before ultimately passing the debt over for recovery.

A key influence on the recovery of the debt is the action taken when the original advance was agreed. For example, did the lender take any security and, if so, is that security realisable? Many lenders have taken court action and found themselves unable to rely on security, previously thought of as providing an alternative source of repayment.

In summary, the subject will provide the lender, or prospective lender, with a framework to operate effectively and lend money safely and profitably, maximising the possibility of repayment by the borrower, or through suitable alternatives, where appropriate.

The structure of the text

This text has been designed to provide the knowledge, understanding and requisite skills to manage the lending requests made by customers effectively, including the repayment or recovery of such advances.

While financial institutions must take a corporate view of lending principles, and in particular that of corporate risk and responsibility, at the shop floor level, individual lenders must understand the framework in which they are lending and the basic tenets by which they must act.

The text is divided into ten topics. In each topic, the content is covered from the point of view of both the lending institution and the individual lender.

The early topics provide a broad framework of the legal and regulatory environment in which lenders operate, so that the lender is fully aware of the implications of making the lending decision. This is followed by an analysis of the different types of customers, their lending requirements and the range of lending services that can be used to satisfy those lending needs.

The general principles of security are then investigated, and applied to different forms of security, whether direct or third party, and whether covering personal or corporate debts.

An overview of the lending process includes a review of the lending cycle, the initial lending decision, the control and monitoring of lending, any early warning signals that the repayment of the debts could be potentially problematic, and the process of debt repayment, recovery or write-off.

The text concludes with the economic and social effects of lending and the importance of responsible lending.

As well as the core knowledge for the module, each topic contains further readings, review questions and activities to help you with your studies. Some topics also contain a case study.

- ◆ **Further reading** – sources that have been selected to give you more information on that particular topic and broaden your knowledge. Further reading is important to enable you to see how your studies fit into the bigger picture of the financial services industry. Further reading can be accessed through the **ifs**' e-library, *KnowledgeBank*.

- ◆ **Review questions** – provided so you can determine your understanding of the topics covered. You should refer back to the core content to check your answers.

- ◆ **Activities** – give you further opportunity to research and understand the key themes of the topic.

- ◆ **Case studies** – encourage you to think further about the application of the concepts covered in the topic. Answers to case study questions are included at the back of the text.

Key terms and paragraphs are highlighted in green boxes within this text.

If you have any feedback regarding these materials please email editorial@ifslearning.ac.uk.

Good luck with your studies.

Module Specification

1. **Title**: Principles of Lending (PRIL)

2. **Start date**: May 2008

3. **Level of unit**: C (within QAA Framework for Higher Education)

4. **Number of credits**: 15 credits

5. **Status**:

   Specialist unit within Applied Diploma – Retail

6. **Recommended prior units**: No mandatory requirements.

7. **Programmes of study to which unit contributes**:

   Applied Diploma in Retailing Financial Services (Applied DFSM® (Retail))

8. **Purpose/rationale/positioning**

   Principles of Lending is a specialist module within an Applied Diploma programme and is intended for students working, or intending to work, in a lending related role. This could include those with direct responsibility for interactions with borrowing customers, or in a support or securities role.

   Lending money is a core skill within the Financial Services industry and as such it is crucial that the customers have a quality experience that can only be provided by staff with an understanding of the subject. Customers expect lenders to have a full and detailed knowledge of the legal and compliance aspect of their roles; these expectations include relevant case and statute law along with the more recent developments in the Banking Code and Business Banking Code, plus the implications of initiatives such as Treating Customers Fairly and Responsible Lending.

   Lenders need to be aware of the diversity of customers that could approach them for the wide range of lending services provided in today's financial market. A lack of understanding of the nature of the customer, or the details of the lending request can result in the lender recommending the wrong product to the customer, or not being able to recover an advance because the lender was not aware of the legal implications of lending to that particular customer type.

   The nature of lending does mean that occasionally the lender will not be able to recover the whole debt from the customer. It is through an appreciation of the risks involved in lending, and an ability to reduce those risks, that providers will be able to make better decisions. A full understanding of the lending cycle undoubtedly reduces the risks. The lending cycle starts with the lending decision (including an analysis of financial information), and includes monitoring and control plus the ability to detect early warning signals, before ultimately, and reluctantly, passing the debt over for recovery.

A key influence on the recovery of the debt is the action taken when the original advance was agreed. For example did the lender take any security and if so is that security realisable? Many lenders have taken court action and found themselves unable to rely on security, previously thought of as providing an alternative source of repayment.

In summary the subject will provide the lender, or prospective lender, with a framework to operate effectively and lend money safely and profitably, maximising the possibility of repayment by the borrower, or through suitable alternatives, where appropriate.

9. **Intended subject specific learning outcomes and, as appropriate, their relationship to programme learning outcomes**

The learning outcomes fall into two main areas to reflect the syllabus content and each outcome will be measured by way of an objective test (see section 12).

On completion of this module, students will be able to:

1. Understand the principles of good lending, including relevant law and codes of practice such as Treating Customers Fairly, Responsible Lending and The Banking Code. Provide an outline of the principles of credit scoring.

2. Understand the nature of different types of borrowers (personal customers, sole traders, partnerships and, limited companies and the lending services that may be of benefit to them.

3. Analyse the borrowing requirements of personal and commercial customers (including the interpretation of financial statements).

4. Understand and apply the features and benefits of the whole range of lending products and services to each customer type and lending situation.

5. Understand the implications and application of the lending cycle, from the lending decision, through lending and control, management of early warning signals to the recovery of debts.

6. Apply the principles of security including land and property, life policies, stocks and shares, guarantees and debentures incorporating fixed and floating charges.

These intended unit learning outcomes contribute to the following programme learning outcomes: A2, A5, A7, A9, A11 and A12.

10. **Intended generic learning outcomes and, as appropriate, their relationship to programme learning outcomes**

On completion of this module students will be able to demonstrate achievement of the following generic learning outcomes:

1. Problem solving and decision taking skills.

2. Ability to learn through reflection on practice and experience.

3. Ability to work with complex material.

4. Ability to analyse problems and identify appropriate solutions.

5. Ability to work and study independently and utilise resources effectively.

These intended generic learning outcomes contribute to the following programme learning outcomes: B2, B3, B4, C4, D2, D3, D4

1. Learning and Teaching

A. Modes of study

There are two approved modes of study for the module: through an approved academic centre and by distance learning.

Academic centre learners

Students enrolled through an academic centre mode will be provided with an approved schedule of classes designed to support students to achieve the learning outcomes of the module.

Distance learners

Distance learners will be given access to a subject tutor, (the key mode of communication is through the My*ifs*ILE forum), for each module to support them through their study session and an *ifs* Higher Education Student Advisor. A distance learner can choose to register for two optional enhancement workshops delivered by *ifs* approved tutors at appointed locations.

B. Learning hours

For a module of study worth 15 credits the total expected study hours are 150 (ie ten hours per credit). The contact hours will be dependent upon the student's mode of study. Distance learners can contact with their appointed *ifs* subject tutor and *ifs* Higher Education Student Advisor. Distance learners opting for enhancement workshops will have two face-to-face sessions of c.6 hours each, evenly spread at appointed dates in each session. Academic centre students will have regular sessions of face-to-face sessions at regular intervals over each session of study. The timing will be dependent on student and local conditions though typically will be c.20 hours (eg: 6 x 3 hour workshops).

C. Learning materials and learning outcomes

Each module has learning materials, activities and resources designed and developed to support students in achieving the learning outcomes. Learning materials and reading links are provided in a folder at registration and each student will have access to the My*ifs*ILE learning environment containing learning activities and discussion forums and the *ifs* *KnowledgeBank* learning resources (an electronic library service). Text and journal readings are provided online. The recommended reading for the module is the *ifs* text *Principles of Lending*.

2. Assessment:

There is one summative assessment component for this unit. Students will sit, at a time of their choosing, an electronically delivered two-hour objective test.

Assessment will focus primarily on the learning outcomes associated with the cognitive skills of knowledge, understanding, analysis and application.

The test comprises 75 questions as follows:

◆ 50 multiple-choice questions that will test knowledge and understanding across the syllabus (1 mark each); and

◆ 5 case studies, each with 5 questions that will test skills of analysis and application (2 marks each).

Total marks available: 100.

13. **Syllabus overview**:

This module has been designed to provide the, knowledge, understanding and requisite skills to effectively manage the lending requests made by customers, including the repayment or recovery of such advances.

The early syllabus sections provide the student with a broad framework of the lending environment, ensuring that the lender is fully aware of the implications of making the lending decision. Students are firstly provided with the legal and compliance environment in which lenders operate, before moving onto an analysis of the different types of customers, their lending requirements and the wide range of lending services that can be used to satisfy those lending needs.

The general principles of security are investigated, such as the features of security, whether direct or third party covering personal or corporate debts.

The syllabus moves on to providing the student with an overview of the whole process . This includes a crucial review of the lending cycle, including the initial lending decision, but also moving on to discuss the control and monitoring of the lending and the early warning signals, that the repayment of the debts could potentially be an issue, before analysing the process of debt recovery.

Syllabus

1. **Lending**

This section of the syllabus introduces the principles and framework of good lending practice. Students will gain an understanding of how lending proposals are evaluated and the reasoned decision-making approach taken.

Its focus is learning outcome 1 and it covers the following:

◆ Attributes of good lending: safety, liquidity and profitability

◆ Principles and analysis of lending

◆ Relevant law, codes of practice and lending policies

◆ Principles of credit scoring: operation, benefits and drawbacks

◆ Treating customers fairly

◆ Responsible lending

2. **Types of Borrower**

This section of the syllabus introduces the nature of different borrowers and types of lending service available to meet the range of customer needs.

Its focus is learning outcome 2 and it covers the following:

◆ Personal borrowers

◆ Sole traders, partnerships (including limited liability partnerships)

◆ Limited companies (legal framework and characteristics of limited companies.

◆ Other borrowers (Including lending to organisations such as clubs and societies, trustees and executors.)

3. **Purpose of borrowing**

This section of the syllabus covers particular types of lending requirements and the finance available to meet the needs that arise as a result of the customer profile.

Its focus is learning outcome 3 and it covers the following:

◆ Working capital

◆ New ventures

◆ Business expansion

◆ Purchase of fixed assets

◆ All forms of consumer finance (including bridging loans and house purchase)

4. **Lending Products**

This section of the syllabus covers the importance of matching products with needs, and it covers the features and benefits of a range of secured and unsecured products.

Its focus is learning outcome 4 and it covers the following:

◆ Overdrafts and current account revolving credit

◆ Loans

◆ Credit cards

◆ Hire purchase and leasing

◆ Factoring

◆ Other sources of finance (including equity finance and government-backed loan guarantee schemes)

5. **The Lending Cycle**

This section of the syllabus covers the life cycle of a lending facility. It will focus on, but is not restricted to, the analysis of a lending proposition and the monitoring and control procedures as part of business management. Consideration will also be given to the actions the lender may decide to take when the customer's ability to repay is under threat.

Its focus is learning outcome 5 and it covers the following:

◆ The lending decision (including interpretation of financial statements)

◆ Monitoring and control (including information sources for review)

◆ Further advances

◆ Early warning management (collections)

◆ Stages of recovery (including the range of insolvency proceedings)

6. **Securities**

This section of the syllabus covers the importance of taking appropriate security cover for both personal and commercial borrowers. Students will be expected to understand the need to perfect security without being required to demonstrate knowledge of the relevant procedures.

Its focus is learning outcome 6 and it covers the following:

◆ General principles of security (including priority, third party or direct)

◆ Land and other property

◆ Life policies

◆ Stocks and shares

◆ Guarantees

◆ Debentures and fixed & floating charge

◆ Advantages and disadvantages of different forms of security

◆ Realisation of security

Topic 1
Introduction to lending principles

Learning outcomes

In this topic, students will be introduced to the basic concepts related to lending, the participants and the activities involved, setting the context for further learning.

Learning areas include:

◆ basic lending concepts;

◆ risk and return;

◆ principles of lending;

◆ attributes of good lending – safety, liquidity and profitability.

Introduction

Lending has been an important economic activity from ancient times. From pawnbroking, to mortgages, to credit derivatives, lending has taken on many shapes and sizes. Today, it is one of the most challenging and significant activities contributing, in large measure, to the effective allocation of resources, and to enabling firms and individuals to achieve their goals and aspirations. Lending plays a significant role in the economy of nations: the availability of credit can determine the extent of a country's economic development.

Lending is determined, to a large extent, by the supply and demand of loanable funds.

The price of a loan will also depend upon other factors, such as the likelihood of the loan being repaid.

Lending is a risky activity and the greater the likelihood of the loan being returned, the greater the likelihood of the lender providing the loan. No lender can be absolutely sure that the money lent will be returned. Prudent lending principles are therefore necessary if lending is to become a successful activity.

1.1 What is 'lending'?

> **Lending** may be defined as the giving of an asset with the expectation that an equivalent value will be returned at a future point of time. A loan is an asset for the lender and a liability for the borrower. To the lender, the loan is an asset that is expected to be repaid along with compensation for the costs and risks of lending. To the borrower the loan is a liability that is required to be repaid along with charges for receiving the benefits of borrowing.

Figure 1.1 The loan

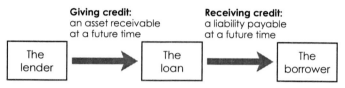

A loan involves the creation of credit. When a loan is granted to a borrower, the lender is the **creditor** and the borrower is the **debtor**.

The amount of the loan is described as the **principal**. The lender will additionally have to be compensated for the costs and risks of lending and the loan will therefore be offered at a price, generally called **interest**.

Interest is the charge for a loan, usually expressed as a percentage of the amount loaned. The price of the loan can also take a number of other forms such as commission, discount, fee, etc.

Islamic banks, which are prohibited from charging interest, obtain their returns in the form of a difference in asset prices: for example, a mortgage lending bank will buy property from borrowers and sell it back to them at a higher price.

Lenders are able to charge interest in a variety of ways. Some examples include:

♦ **fixed interest**, where interest is fixed for a specified period;

♦ **variable interest**, where interest varies in relation to an underlying reference rate such as the base rate or LIBOR (the London Inter Bank Offered Rate). The Standard Variable Rate (SVR) is the standard rate of interest that lenders use and it is the rate to which a borrower is automatically switched when any fixed or initial offer period expires. It is usually set at around 1–2% higher than the Bank of England base rate to which it is linked and therefore varies with changes in the base rate;

♦ **capped interest**, where interest is subject to a specified ceiling;

♦ **simple interest**, where there is no compounding of interest;

♦ **compound interest**, where interest is calculated on interest at periodic intervals and added to the principal.

In *Yourell v Hibernian Bank Ltd* [1918], it was held that charging compound interest was a 'usual and perfectly legitimate mode of dealing between banker and customer'.

> The **annual equivalent rate (AER)** or **effective annual rate (EAR)** is the annualised rate of interest, including the compounding effect of charging interest more frequently than once a year. The more frequently interest is applied in a year, the higher will be the effective annual interest rate. Unlike the **annual percentage rate (APR)**, it does not include charges and fees, and can therefore be misleading when it comes to calculating the cost of a loan. The APR is the annualised interest rate, including both the effect of interest compounding and the impact of other (non-interest) charges. (*Note:* in the USA the APR does not show the effect of compounding.)

In addition to interest, lenders charge **fees** to cover their expenses and to generate profit. Some examples include:

◆ an **arrangement fee** at the time of loan approval;

◆ a **valuation fee** for any valuation of assets;

◆ **legal fees** in relation to arranging the loan;

◆ a **higher lending charge (HLC)**, formerly known as a *mortgage indemnity guarantee (MIG)*, levied when the amount borrowed exceeds a given percentage of the value of the property and used by the lender to arrange insurance for protection against loan default.

Earnings by way of interest and fees are shown on the income side of a lender's profit and loss account, and costs of borrowing funds and administering loans are shown on the expenditure side. Earnings from loans constitute a major part of banks' operating income, and lending continues to be a core part of the business of banking despite the growth of alternative financial activities.

> **Gearing** or **leverage** is the use of credit or borrowed funds to improve the rate of return from an investment. A high level of gearing or leverage indicates a high proportion of debt in a company's capital structure.

Loans are assets for the lender and are shown on the asset side of a lending organisation's balance sheet. Loans require the provision of more capital than some other forms of asset. The Basel Accord specifies a minimum capital asset ratio of 8%. Banks have therefore been attempting to remove loans from the asset side of the balance sheet by a process of bundling them and converting them into securities, which can be traded in the secondary market. Such securities are sold off to investors and are therefore no longer required to be retained on the balance sheet and are converted to off-balance sheet items. For example, **collateralised loan obligations (CLOs)** and **collateralised debt obligations (CDOs)** are loans such as mortgages backed by assets, which are packaged and then broken up into securities and sold to investors such as pension funds, hedge funds, special investment vehicles (SIVs) and other investors looking for a return from these assets.

Traditionally, financial institutions have acted as intermediaries and have borrowed funds from those who have surplus money and lent these funds to those who are in need of funds for consumption or investment.

> **Financial intermediation** is the process whereby the financial intermediary borrows from savers and lends to borrowers. **Financial disintermediation** takes place when borrowers and lenders no longer rely on the financial intermediary, but instead lend and borrow directly from each other.

1.2 An overview of lending in the UK

A **market** is generated when buyers and sellers get together for the purpose of carrying out their transactions. A *financial market* is a market within which financial products are bought and sold. A *credit market* is a financial market within which money is lent and borrowed.

Lending in the UK ranges from mainstream lending undertaken by banks and other financial institutions, to social lending undertaken by individuals to friends and family, and on websites such as Zopa. Lending in the UK can be broadly divided under the following three categories.

1. **Commercial lending:**

    – to ultra-prime and near-prime borrowers;

    – to sub-prime or high-risk borrowers.

2. **Not-for-profit lending:**

    – by the credit unions and other community-based lenders to those on low incomes;

    – by the government's social lending operation the Social Fund, which provides interest-free loans to benefit recipients and those on the lowest incomes.

The mainstrean commercial lenders are listed below:

♦ banks (both domestic and foreign-owned), including retail and investment banks;

♦ card issuers;

♦ building societies;

♦ funds, eg hedge funds, sovereign funds;

♦ others, eg private equity firms.

Mainstream lenders range from direct and multi-product lenders, to remote and single product lenders such as overseas card issuers. They offer a range of services via a range of delivery channels, including branch, telephone, ATM, card and Internet.

♦ **Retail banks** usually deal with a large number of customers and small value transactions. A retail bank is a financial institution that allows its customers to deal with retail transactions on a mass scale, eg current accounts, personal loans, mortgages, credit cards. (The same bank is likely to undertake both retail and wholesale activity, and is labelled as 'retail' or 'investment' depending upon its dominant activity.) Retail banks such as Barclays, Lloyds TSB, HBOS, for example, usually have their own investment banking arms, eg Barclays Capital.

◆ Investment is the purchase of an asset with the expectation that it will generate a return or appreciate in value in the future. An **investment bank** is a financial institution that helps its customers to raise money for investment in a variety of ways, eg raising capital, handling mergers and acquisitions, dealing in securities. Investment banks are also sometimes known as **wholesale banks** because they deal with fewer customers, smaller number of transactions and larger sums of money. Such banks include Goldman Sachs, JP Morgan, UBS, Merrill Lynch and Morgan Stanley.

◆ **Credit card issuers** comprise banks or businesses that authorise the holder to buy goods or services on credit, and include remote lenders such as US card issuers (Ellison et al, 2006). GE Capital and Capital One are two examples.

◆ **Building societies** are mutually owned by borrowers and savers. They operate under the Building Societies Acts 1977 and 1986 but are able to offer better prices, because they do not have any shareholders who expect a return for their investment. Their traditional focus is mortgages for owner-occupied residential property. Nationwide, Britannia, Leeds and Holbeck are all well-known building societies.

◆ Historically, **Hedge funds** were so named because of their investment strategies to limit and protect against risk. Now, these funds are more speculative than many other funds and aim to maximise profits, which involves exposure to a greater level of risk. These funds are highly leveraged, and borrow heavily from banks and other institutions. Some of these funds are set up by banks themselves, eg George Soros' Quantum Fund.

◆ **Private equity firms** borrow money from banks in order to finance or buy up companies. Many of them are highly leveraged, and borrow heavily from banks and other institutions. Some of these firms are set up by banks themselves.

◆ **Sovereign states or countries** will need money for various reasons and have borrowed from banks; they will also have been lending to banks.

Lenders and borrowers are diverse. While the principles of lending will broadly remain the same for all categories, the main focus of this text will be on the mainstream lending firms that undertake commercial lending.

1.3   Risk and return

Risk can be considered to be the raw material for firms that undertake the business of lending. As Matthews and Thompson (2005) observe: 'The business of banking involves risk. Banks make profit by taking risk and managing risk'. Risk and return are directly related to each other: the higher the risk, the higher the return that will be required by the lender.

Mispriced loans, or low-cost loans to high-risk borrowers, can lead to serious problems for lenders, as evidenced by the 2007/08 credit crunch in financial markets.

1.3.1 What is risk?

Risk is the probability of exposure to loss. Risk is 'the probability that the value of a financial asset or return will be less than its expected value' (Pilbeam, 2005). The greater the uncertainty or variability, the greater will be the risk. Therefore, one fundamental measure of risk is the volatility or standard deviation (the square root of the variance) of net cash flows of an investment.

Risk can be considered to be the combination of **impact** (the potential harm that could be caused) and **probability** (the likelihood of the particular issue or event occurring) (FSA, 2006b). We can formulate this as:

$$\text{RISK} = \frac{\text{IMPACT}}{\text{of the problem if it occurs}} \times \frac{\text{PROBABILITY}}{\text{of the problem occurring}}$$

1.3.2 What are the risks in lending?

Lenders of money are risk takers. A lender who never loses any money is being overcautious and missing opportunities for profit, while a lender who loses money frequently is depleting the profit made on loans that are repaid.

Lending involves a number of risks including:

◆ credit risk;

◆ interest-rate risk;

◆ currency risk;

◆ country risk;

◆ contagion risk.

Credit risk or **default risk** is one of the primary risks in lending: it is the probability of a loss occurring due to the failure of a borrower or obligor to meet contractual debt obligations. It is the risk that the borrower will default in the repayment of the principal or interest and other fees payable or both. It is the risk that the obligor, in respect of a particular asset, will default in full or in part on its obligations to the lender in relation to that asset. It is the risk that an asset or a loan becomes irrecoverable in the case of outright default or the risk of delay in the servicing of the loan. Credit risk is 'the potential that a bank borrower or counterparty will fail to meet its obligations in accordance with agreed terms' (Basel, 2000). In such situations, the present value of the asset declines, thereby undermining the solvency of the lender.

Credit risk can be borrower specific or systematic. **Borrower-specific credit risk** is the risk of default of the borrower specific types of project risk taken by that borrower. **Systematic credit risk** is the risk of default associated with general economy wide or macro conditions affecting all borrowers. Borrower-specific credit risk can be further subdivided as **standalone risk**, which refers to the risk of loans as independent assets, and **portfolio risk**, which measures the risk of the portfolio or group of loans held by the lender. Holding loans that are correlated increases portfolio risk, while holding a diversified portfolio of assets could reduce this type of risk – but a 'lesson to be learnt is that spreading risk does not eliminate it' (Heaney, 2007).

Interest-rate risk is the risk that the value of an asset will change due to a change in the level of interest rates; the cost of funding a loan might then be higher than the return from the loan.

Currency risk arises from the change in the price of one currency against another. Lenders might wish to borrow in a currency in relation to which interest rates are low, convert it into another currency with higher interest rates and then lend in that currency. Any increase in the borrowed currency and decrease in the currency that is being lent can result in losses for the lender.

Country risk is the risk that a country is not able, or willing, to honour its financial commitments.

Contagion risk is the risk that difficulties experienced by one or more lenders will spill over to, or 'contaminate', other lenders or the financial system as a whole. Contagion risk is also known as **systemic risk**. Systemic risk is so known because the risk affects the entire financial system as a whole, rather than any particular participant or participants. The turmoil in financial markets in 2007 for example, is attributed to difficulties in the US sub-prime lending market. Because banks lend to each other, and make payments to and on behalf of each other, there is a possibility that financial difficulties can be contagious and be passed on to other institutions and markets. Generally, the central bank is held to be an important player in such circumstances and is required to act as **lender of last resort**, that is, to be prepared to lend money and offer liquidity whatever the situation – although the price of that lending will be of the central bank's choosing.

It will be relevant to note some of the recent developments in the credit markets, as follows.

♦ **Rise in the number of players** – while, traditionally, banks have dominated the lending arena, many new and active players have emerged today, eg pension funds, insurance companies, private equity firms, SIVs, etc.

♦ **A rise in the use of technology to manage risk** – computer models that are good in theory may fail to work effectively when faced with real market crisis and theoretically flawed computer models could accentuate risk profiles.

♦ **The increased repackaging and redistribution of risk** – financial institutions are able to handle greater volumes of risk by taking them off their balance sheets via securitisation and other measures.

♦ **Increased globalisation** means that financial crises in one country can spread globally within a very short time.

♦ **An increased lack of transparency** means that it is not always clear who is holding the credit risk. This can, in turn, lead to loss of confidence in the financial markets.

♦ **The unwillingness of organisations to recognise and acknowledge the extent of risk** – this could be due to diverse reasons, eg dependence of personal bonuses on bank performance, and the impact of credit losses on the size of bonuses and jobs.

Lenders need to manage risk. Traditional financial regulations developed standardised control systems, based on external assessments made by credit rating and other agencies. The globalised economic environment, however, requires more sophisticated and adaptive credit risk management systems, which, in turn, might accentuate, rather than alleviate risk. Managing lending risk is thus one of the biggest challenges that lenders need to confront if they are to manage the lending function profitably and safely.

1.3.3 The risk–return trade-off

There is a trade-off between risk and return. The potential return rises with an increase in risk. Low levels of uncertainty (low risk) are associated with low potential returns, whereas high levels of uncertainty (high risk) are associated with high potential returns. Lenders will need to control and manage risk by:

◆ identifying risk;

◆ measuring risk;

◆ mitigating risk;

◆ monitoring risk.

Figure 1.2   The management of risk

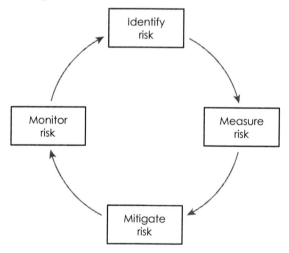

Risk management strategies will be discussed in Topic 6 when the lending cycle is being considered in detail.

1.4   Attributes of good lending

A lender needs to balance a number of conflicting objectives in order to achieve required goals. These objectives can be conflicting and contradictory and a fine balancing act is necessary. Some of the major objectives are:

◆ safety;

◆ liquidity;

◆ profitability.

The lender would like the money lent to be liquid, profitable and safe. It may, however, be necessary to balance the needs of one against the other and to arrive at some kind of a compromise between these conflicting objectives in order to optimise the lending activity.

1.4.1 Safety

The lender needs to ensure that funds lent are safe and that the lender's own financial position is sound. Safety, when applied to an advance, is an understanding that the borrower has the legal capacity to borrow, and to provide security should this be required.

1.4.2 Liquidity

Liquidityis the ability of the borrower to meet repayments when they fall due. In the case of a personal loan this would be from monthly or weekly income, and for a business from cash generated in the normal course of trade.

1.4.3 Profitability

Profitability is measured in terms of the income generated by the advance in terms of interest and fees and its proper reflection of the risk involved.

The top UK banks made record profits in 2006 as indicated in Table 1.1.

Table 1.1 Profits earned by top UK banks in 2006

The combined profits of £32bn made by top UK banks in 2006 exceeded the gross domestic product (GDP) of Luxembourg	
Bank	**Profits (£bn)**
Barclays	5.2
Lloyds TSB	3.47
Royal Bank of Scotland	7.94
Halifax Bank of Scotland	4.8
Hong Kong and Shanghai Banking Corporation	11.5

Source: BBC

It now appears, however, that these profits might have been earned at the cost of decreased safety and liquidity. The profitability in 2007 is expected to be much reduced as fears of a liquidity shortage grips the financial system.

Profitability is the measure of success of the lender in undertaking lending operations, but it is subject to also meeting the conflicting requirements of liquidity and safety, as indicated in Figure 1.3.

Figure 1.3 Lending objectives

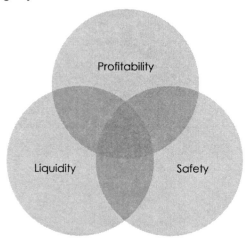

1.5 The principles of lending

Principles may be defined as generally accepted rules for action or conduct. Lenders will wish to adopt generally accepted principles of lending that might enable them to maximise the return from lending and minimise the possibility of loss. Developing and adopting lending principles is not an exact science. Lending principles have evolved over a period of time and will continue to evolve in the future. Individual lenders will need to adapt these principles to suit their individual needs. As a text directed towards learning about the principles of lending, it will be worth noting, at the very outset, key areas of credit risk management and the key principles of credit risk management identified and developed by the Basel Committee.

1.5.1 Areas of credit risk management

The Basel Committee sets out sound lending practices that address the following **four areas** of credit risk management.

1. Establishing an appropriate credit risk environment.

2. Operating under a sound credit granting process.

3. Maintaining an appropriate credit administration, measurement and monitoring process.

4. Ensuring adequate controls over credit risk.

1.5.2 Principles for evaluating a bank's credit management system

Within these four areas, 17 principles of good lending have been identified and discussed by the Basel Committee.

The principles set out below should be used in evaluating a lender's credit management system.

A. Establishing an appropriate credit risk environment

Principle 1: The board of directors should have responsibility for approving and periodically (at least annually) reviewing the credit risk strategy and significant credit risk policies of the bank. The strategy should reflect the bank's tolerance for risk and the level of profitability the bank expects to achieve for incurring various credit risks.

Principle 2: Senior management should have responsibility for implementing the credit risk strategy approved by the board of directors and for developing policies and procedures for identifying, measuring, monitoring and controlling credit risk. Such policies and procedures should address credit risk in all of the bank's activities and at both the individual credit and portfolio levels.

Principle 3: Banks should identify and manage credit risk inherent in all products and activities. Banks should ensure that the risks of products and activities new to them are subject to adequate risk management procedures and controls before being introduced or undertaken, and approved in advance by the board of directors or its appropriate committee.

B. Operating under a sound credit granting process

Principle 4: Banks must operate within sound, well-defined credit-granting criteria. These criteria should include a clear indication of the bank's target market and a thorough understanding of the borrower or counterparty, as well as the purpose and structure of the credit, and its source of repayment.

Principle 5: Banks should establish overall credit limits at the level of individual borrowers and counterparties, and groups of connected counterparties that aggregate in a comparable and meaningful manner different types of exposures, both in the banking and trading book and on and off the balance sheet.

Principle 6: Banks should have a clearly-established process in place for approving new credits as well as the amendment, renewal and re-financing of existing credits.

Principle 7: All extensions of credit must be made on an arm's-length basis. In particular, credits to related companies and individuals must be authorised on an exception basis, monitored with particular care and other appropriate steps taken to control or mitigate the risks of non-arm's length lending.

C. Maintaining an appropriate credit administration, measurement and monitoring process

Principle 8: Banks should have in place a system for the ongoing administration of their various credit risk-bearing portfolios.

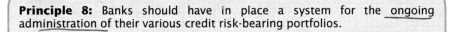

Principle 9: Banks must have in place a system for monitoring the condition of individual credits, including determining the adequacy of provisions and reserves.

Principle 10: Banks are encouraged to develop and utilise an internal risk rating system in managing credit risk. The rating system should be consistent with the nature, size and complexity of a bank's activities.

Principle 11: Banks must have information systems and analytical techniques that enable management to measure the credit risk inherent in all on- and off-balance sheet activities. The management information system should provide adequate information on the composition of the credit portfolio, including identification of any concentrations of risk.

Principle 12: Banks must have in place a system for monitoring the overall composition and quality of the credit portfolio.

Principle 13: Banks should take into consideration potential future changes in economic conditions when assessing individual credits and their credit portfolios, and should assess their credit risk exposures under stressful conditions.

D. Ensuring adequate controls over credit risk

Principle 14: Banks must establish a system of independent, ongoing assessment of the bank's credit risk management processes and the results of such reviews should be communicated directly to the board of directors and senior management.

Principle 15: Banks must ensure that the credit-granting function is being properly managed and that credit exposures are within levels consistent with prudential standards and internal limits. Banks should establish and enforce internal controls and other practices to ensure that exceptions to policies, procedures and limits are reported in a timely manner to the appropriate level of management for action.

Principle 16: Banks must have a system in place for early remedial action on deteriorating credits, managing problem credits and similar workout situations.

E. The role of supervisors

Principle 17: Supervisors should require that banks have an effective system in place to identify, measure, monitor and control credit risk as part of an overall approach to risk management. Supervisors should conduct an independent evaluation of a bank's strategies, policies, procedures and practices related to the granting of credit and the ongoing management of the portfolio. Supervisors should consider setting prudential limits to restrict bank exposures to single borrowers or groups of connected counterparties.

Source: Basel, 2000.

These principles will be revisited when each component of the lending activity is discussed. For example the principles for credit granting will be discussed in Topic 6, while the principles of credit administration and monitoring will be discussed in Topic 9.

Conclusion

Lending is the giving of an asset with the expectation that an equivalent value will be returned at a future point of time.

Lending in the UK ranges from mainstream lending undertaken by banks and other financial institutions to social lending undertaken by individuals to friends and family and on websites.

Credit risk is the possibility that a borrower will fail to meet repayment obligations in accordance with agreed terms. Risk and return are directly related to each other; the higher the risk the higher the return that will be required by the lender.

A lender needs to balance a number of conflicting objectives in order to achieve required goals. Some of the major objectives are safety, liquidity and profitability.

Lenders will wish to adopt generally accepted principles of lending that might enable them to maximise the return from lending and minimise the possibility of loss. It will be worth noting, at the very outset, key areas of credit risk management and the key principles of credit risk management identified and developed by the Basel Committee.

Further reading

Ellison, A., Collard, S. and Forster, R. (2006) *Illegal lending in the UK*, London, DTI.

Financial Services Authority (2007) *Treating Customers Fairly – Culture*, London: FSA.

Matthews, K. and Thompson, J. (2005) *The Economics of Banking*, Chichester, John Wiley and Sons Ltd.

***ifs** KnowledgeBank* Subject Gateway (2007), 'The US sub-prime lending crisis and its global impact on Financial Services'.

Topic 1

Review questions, activity and case study

The following review questions, activity and case study are designed to increase your understanding of the material you have just studied.

◆ The **review questions** are designed so that you can check your understanding of this topic.

◆ Completion of the **activity** will give you further opportunity to research and understand, in more depth, the themes running through this topic.

◆ The **case study** encourages you to think further about the application of the content of this topic.

The answers to the questions and case study are provided at the end of these learning materials. Please note that the activity is open-ended and therefore a suitable 'answer' may not be provided.

Review questions

?

1. What are the various risks that lending might entail?

2. What is 'credit risk'?

3. What is the relationship between risk and return?

4. What are the attributes of good lending?

5. What are the four major areas of credit risk management identified by the Basel Committee?

Activity

Activity 1

> Visit the website of Bank for International Settlements at www.bis.org Locate and read the article *Principles for the Management of Credit Risk* at http://www.bis.org/publ/bcbs75.pdf.

Case study – turmoil in the credit markets – 2007

Financial markets have been in turmoil in 2007. Liquidity has dried up. Lenders are unwilling or unable to lend to one another in the manner to which they had been accustomed.

The origin of the recent squeeze in credit availability is traced to the US sub-prime market, in which more than half the borrowers are reported to have lied, or have been encouraged to lie, about their income. Sub-prime lending is lending offered at higher rates of interest to borrowers with poor credit history. Lenders were less than assiduous in credit appraisal, because they felt that the loans granted would very quickly be removed from their balance sheets by conversion into debt securities and sold off to eager investors. Loans were thus transferred into the hands of insurers and other investors, who were motivated by the prospect of high returns but who were not necessarily the people best equipped to evaluate the risk that was being taken on their books.

When difficulties in the sub-prime market gave rise to borrower defaults, the problems were compounded by a fall in house prices and an increase in borrowing rates that in turn trapped more borrowers in debt that they could not afford to repay.

Lenders who had considered themselves to be insulated against sub-prime borrower default risk found themselves nonetheless exposed to the risk, via complex interrelationships that characterise present day financial markets. Even if they did not have exposure to these borrowers directly, it appeared that some of the special investment vehicles (SIVs) that they had set up had gained exposure through their investment activities.

Funds dried up, and lenders were wary of lending to each other lest they ran out of liquidity themselves.

Aggressive lenders found themselves particularly vulnerable. Northern Rock, for example, had lent long-term funds towards mortgages and had funded these mortgages by cheap short term borrowing from the wholesale money markets. While this high risk strategy paid off with high profits when wholesale funds were plentiful, it ceased to work when the credit markets seized up. The bank was forced to approach the Bank of England as lender of last resort. By December 2007, the Bank of England's commitment to Northern Rock had exceeded £55bn, indicating that the taxpayer was effectively underwriting the risks taken by the lending banker.

Northern Rock's strategy of short-term borrowing and long-term long-term was highly profitable under conditions of credit boom. But when funds ran dry, the bank faced insolvency. Thus it was found that **profitability had run counter to liquidity requirements**.

Banks have been queuing up to announce loan write-offs and provisions for bad debts. Here are some of the headlines made by banks in 2007.

◆ Swiss Bank 'UBS AG will write off a further $10 billion (£5 billion) on losses in the US sub prime lending market' – Associated Press, 10 December 2007.

◆ 'Lloyds TSB reveals that bad debt linked to the US sub-prime mortgage crisis will cost it £200m' – BBC, 10 December 2007.

◆ 'Royal Bank of Scotland warns it will write off about £1.25 billion because of exposure to the US sub-prime market' – BBC, 6 December 2007.

◆ 'Canadian Banks write off $2.1 billion in US Sub Prime mortgages' – The Bankwatch, 17 November 2007.

◆ 'Barclays calculates £1.3 billion sub-prime loss' – *The Guardian*, 16 November 2007.

◆ HSBC's 'misadventures in the US mortgage market have forced to it to write off up to $11 billion (£5.7 billion)' *The Independent*, 5 March 2007.

There is also exposure to sub-prime borrowers in this country. High-risk borrowers yielded high returns because they were prepared to borrow at high rates of interest. When they found themselves unable to repay the loan or interest or both, however, high yields were converted to large losses. Thus it was found that **profitability had run counter to safety in lending**.

1 What seems to be the root cause of the turmoil in the credit markets in 2007?

2 What is 'sub prime lending'?

3 What was the high risk high profit strategy of Northern Rock that backfired?

4 What can be the impact of poor lending decisions?

5 What are the lessons here for lenders?

© *ifs* School of Finance 2008

Topic 2
The legal and regulatory environment

Learning outcomes

By the end of this topic, students should be able to understand the legal and regulatory environment in which lending takes place.

Learning areas include:

◆ relevant statutes;

◆ codes of practice;

◆ Ombudsmen;

◆ treating customers fairly (TCF).

2.1　The legal and regulatory framework

In order to be effective, the lending function needs to be regulated by the lending organisations themselves as well as by independent authorities. While regulation is able at least partially to overcome market imperfections, powerful regulators can become subject to undue influence from both politicians and the banks that are being regulated (Barth et al, 2007). Excessive regulation can curb credit development and growth, while inadequate regulation can lead to widespread loss of confidence in the credit markets. The level of competition will vary depending upon the regulatory, economic and other environmental factors. Even within the same country competition can vary within different sub-markets (Cruickshank, 2000; Matthrews et al, 2007). In the UK, it has been suggested that individual sub-markets, such as that relating to credit cards, have deteriorated while others such as mortgages, have seen a strong increase in competition (Heffernan, 2002). Lending firms will have to adapt their lending strategy depending upon the level and nature of competition encountered.

It is necessary to understand the regulatory environment in order to be able to develop effective lending policies and practices. The following are some of the recent trends that have been identified in the UK lending environment.

◆ Increased deregulation has encouraged a range of organisations to undertake lending activity.

◆ The eagerness to embrace market principles has tended to encourage a more lax regulatory approach.

♦ The blurring of organisational boundaries has resulted in overlapping credit activities, increasing the need for more consistent regulation.

♦ Some non-bank originators of credit have often evaded scrutiny. There is a need for more encompassing supervision of credit markets.

♦ Increased competition has given rise to pressures on profit margins.

♦ Increased demand for credit has led to unprecedented levels of debt.

♦ The increased borrower sophistication has put pressure on lenders to develop more and more complex products.

♦ Increased demand for complex forms of debt financing have led to a certain opaqueness in the credit markets.

♦ Increased borrower range includes hedge funds, private equity firms and financial sponsors wishing to make a splash in the credit market through acquisitions and private placements.

♦ All time high levels in lending and massive increases in leverage levels seem to be heading towards a correction.

The UK has adopted a tripartite system of regulation. The **Memorandum of Understanding for Financial Stability**, published jointly by HM Treasury, the Bank of England and the Financial Services Authority (FSA), sets out a framework for monitoring, assessing and co-ordinating the authorities' responses to financial stability risks. The process is overseen by the **Tripartite Standing Committee**, comprising:

♦ the Chancellor of the Exchequer;

♦ the Governor of the Bank of England;

♦ the Chairman of the FSA.

The Memorandum sets out the roles and responsibilities of each authority.

♦ The Bank of England contributes to the maintenance of the stability of the financial system as a whole.

♦ The FSA is responsible for the authorisation and supervision of financial institutions, and for supervising financial markets and securities clearing and settlement systems, and for regulatory policy in these areas.

♦ HM Treasury has responsibility for the overall institutional structure of regulation and the legislation that governs it.

This tripartite system has sometimes given rise to accusations of a lack of accountability and scope for 'passing the buck'.

There are also other bodies that have an impact on the lending function. For example, the **Office of Fair Trading (OFT)** is a non-ministerial government department established by statute in 1973, and is the UK's consumer and competition authority. The OFT aims to make markets work well for consumers by:

♦ encouraging businesses to comply with competition and consumer law and to improve their trading practices through self-regulation;

♦ discouraging offenders;

- studying markets and recommending action where required;

- empowering consumers with the knowledge and skills to make informed choices and to get the best value from markets, and helping them to resolve problems with suppliers through Consumer Direct.

Source: OFT, 2007

Relevant law needs to be constantly kept in view by those who exercise the lending function. Some of the more important pieces of legislation in the UK are discussed below.

2.1.1 The Financial Services and Markets Act (FSMA) 2000

The effect of Part III of the Bank of England Act 1998 was to transfer the Bank of England's supervisory functions to the FSA. The effect of the Financial Services and Markets Act (FSMA) 2000 was to constitute the FSA as a super-regulator, with powers to regulate insurance, investment business and banking.

The FSA's regulatory processes include:

- authorisation;

- supervision; and

- enforcement.

Under FSMA 2000, a professional firm wishing to provide mainstream financial services will need to achieve authorisation from the FSA. Subsequent to authorisation, the firm will be regulated by the FSA and must comply with the FSA's Handbook of rules and guidance. FSMA 2000 also established the **Financial Services and Markets Tribunal**, and created a single compensation and ombudsman scheme called the **Financial Ombudsman Service (FOS)**.

The FSA's regulatory objectives under FSMA 2000 are:

- market confidence;

- consumer awareness;

- consumer protection;

- fighting financial crime.

2.1.2 The Consumer Credit Acts 1974 and 2006

The **Consumer Credit Act 1974** was enacted in order to protect non-corporate consumers and covered a range of consumer credit up to a limit of £15,000, later increased to £25,000. The limit was removed by the Consumer Credit Act 2006.

By definition, companies are excluded from the remit of the Act. Other exemptions include high net worth debtors and some businesses.

Credit agreements can take place between the creditor and debtor, or between the creditor, debtor and suppliers; credit can be extended as a fixed sum (eg a loan) or a running account (eg an overdraft). The lender can either specify the purpose for which the credit has to be used or allow the debtor to use it for any purpose (unrestricted).

There can be eight basic combinations of credit agreement:

1. debtor–creditor/restricted use/fixed sum;

2. debtor–creditor/unrestricted use/fixed sum;

3. debtor–creditor/restricted use/running account;

4. debtor–creditor/unrestricted use/running account;

5. debtor–creditor–supplier/restricted use/fixed sum;

6. debtor–creditor–supplier/unrestricted use/fixed sum;

7. debtor–creditor–supplier/unrestricted use/running account;

8. debtor–creditor–supplier/unrestricted use/running account.

In addition, credit agreements may be cancellable, non-cancellable, modifying, multiple or credit token. A credit card, for example is a credit token.

The **Consumer Credit Act 2006** amends the Consumer Credit Act 1974, with a view to protecting consumers, and to creating a fairer and more competitive credit market.

Some of the significant features of these Acts are indicated below.

♦ Businesses that provide credit need to obtain a licence from the Office of Fair Trading (OFT), which will be required to ensure that applicants are fit to hold a licence and to monitor ongoing conduct.

♦ Consumer credit agreements need to indicate the rights and duties of the consumer and the true cost of the credit or the 'total charge for credit'.

♦ Consumer protection is extended to all consumer credit; the financial limit that capped protection at loans of £25,000 has been abolished.

♦ Section 75 of the Consumer Credit Act 1974 establishes the principle of 'connected lender liability', whereby credit card issuers are liable for payments for products and services with between £100 and £30,000, individually and jointly with suppliers if a consumer has a valid claim against the supplier for misrepresentation or breach of contract relating to goods or services bought with a credit card. The consumer can make a claim against the credit card issuer as well as, or instead of, the supplier. In *Office of Fair Trading v Lloyds Bank plc, Tesco Personal Finance Ltd, and American Express Services Europe Ltd* [2006] it was held that s 75 protection will cover purchases made on a credit card abroad as well as in the UK (Saxby, 2006); this was upheld by a House of Lords ruling in 2007.

♦ Alternative dispute resolution (ADR) extends the ombudsman scheme under FSMA 2000 to cover licensees under the Consumer Credit Act 1974. If a consumer has complained to a consumer credit business and not received a satisfactory result, they will be able to make complaints to an ADR scheme run by the Financial Ombudsman Service, which will apply to all consumer credit licensees.

♦ There is a new 'unfair relationships between creditors and debtors' test. The previous 'extortionate credit' test is replaced with a test based on unfairness.

The court may make an order in connection with a credit agreement if it determines that the relationship between the creditor and the debtor arising out of the agreement is unfair to the debtor because of any of the terms of the agreement, or the way in which the creditor has exercised or enforced any of their rights, or any other relevant action or inaction by the creditor. This unfair relationships test will apply to all new credit agreements made on or after 6 April 2007, and also to any existing agreements that continue to exist beyond 6 April 2008.

2.1.3 The Insolvency Acts 1986, 1994 and 2000

The UK Insolvency Acts deal with various aspects of the insolvency of individuals, small firms and large corporates that will impact upon the activity of lenders, which will be covered in detail in Topic 9. The main purpose of the Insolvency Act 2000 was to create a moratorium procedure for small companies in financial difficulty. It also provides for streamlining the procedure for disqualifying directors under the Company Directors Disqualification Act 1986.

There have been further amendments to the law about insolvency by statutes such as the Enterprise Act 2002.

2.1.4 Enterprise Act 2002

The Enterprise Act 2002 covers many aspects relating to fair trading and the probity of company directors. For the lender, the most important changes relate to its amendment of the Insolvency Act 1986.

The Act's provisions on corporate insolvency and the abolition of Crown preference came into force on 15 September 2003. The individual insolvency provisions came into force on 1 April 2004.

The following summarises the insolvency provisions in the Enterprise Act 2002 that might be relevant to a lender.

◆ **Company.**

- The procedure of administration has been made more accessible. Holders of floating charges, companies and directors of those companies are able to appoint an administrator simply by filing a notice of appointment at court, without a court application and hearing. In specified circumstances, they will have to give notice before filing such a notice.

- The ability of lenders who hold pre-existing floating charges to appoint an administrative receiver has been restricted.

- Powers to extend certain insolvency proceedings to foreign companies, industrial and provident societies, and friendly societies have been introduced.

◆ **Individual.**

- There is now an automatic discharge of nearly all bankrupts after a maximum of 12 months.

- Bankruptcy restrictions orders (BROs) have been introduced to protect the public from bankrupts whose conduct before, and during, bankruptcy has been found to be culpable.

- The Official Receiver (OR) has been enabled to act as nominee and supervisor of new fast-track Individual Voluntary Arrangements (IVAs) begun after a bankruptcy order has been made.

- The period during which a trustee may deal with a bankrupt's interest in the sole or principal home of the bankrupt, the bankrupt's spouse or a former spouse has been limited to three years. After this period the home will revert back to the bankrupt and will no longer form part of the bankruptcy estate.

◆ The Crown's preferential rights in all insolvencies have been abolished, and unsecured creditors have become major beneficiaries.

The Act distinguishes between responsible and reckless businesses that go bankrupt. Those deemed to be responsible will be given the opportunity to have a fresh start and, if they co-operate with the Official Receiver, they will be discharged from their debts and released from any restrictions after a maximum of 12 months. Those who are considered to have brought about their bankruptcy through reckless or irresponsible behaviour will face restrictions of between two and 15 years under a new bankruptcy restrictions order system.

2.1.5 The Data Protection Act 1998

The Data Protection Act 1998 expanded on the Data Protection Act 1984 and was an implementation of Directive 95/46/EC. The Data Protection Registrar was renamed the Data Protection Commissioner, which was changed again to Office of the Information Commissioner with the passing of the Freedom of Information Act 2000.

The Data Protection Act 1998 provides for the regulation of the processing of information relating to individuals; it creates rights for those who have their data stored and responsibilities for those who store or collect personal data.

Eight **data protection principles** are set out in Part I of Schedule 1 of the Act. They are set out as follows.

1. Personal data shall be processed fairly and lawfully and, in particular, shall not be processed unless:

    a. at least one of the conditions in Schedule 2 is met, and

    b. in the case of sensitive personal data, at least one of the conditions in Schedule 3 is also met.

2. Personal data shall be obtained only for one or more specified and lawful purposes, and shall not be further processed in any manner incompatible with that purpose or those purposes.

3. Personal data shall be adequate, relevant and not excessive in relation to the purpose or purposes for which they are processed.

4. Personal data shall be accurate and, where necessary, kept up to date.

5. Personal data processed for any purpose or purposes shall not be kept for longer than is necessary for that purpose or those purposes.

6. Personal data shall be processed in accordance with the rights of data subjects under this Act.

7. Appropriate technical and organisational measures shall be taken against unauthorised or unlawful processing of personal data and against accidental loss or destruction of, or damage to, personal data.

8. Personal data shall not be transferred to a country or territory outside the European Economic Area unless that country or territory ensures an adequate level of protection for the rights and freedoms of data subjects in relation to the processing of personal data.

Source: Data Protection Act 1998

The person whose data is processed has the right to:

◆ view the data against payment of a small fee;

◆ request that incorrect information is corrected;

◆ require that data is not used in a way that causes damage or distress;

◆ require that their data is not used for direct marketing.

2.2 Codes of practice

Banking codes are voluntary, and attempt to set minimum standards for the way in which banks and other financial services providers should treat their customers. All of the major high street banks, building societies and card issuers subscribe to the UK's Banking Codes. There are, however, a few smaller institutions that do not.

Copies of the Banking Codes can be obtained from any institution that has signed up to it or via the website of the Banking Code Standards Board at www.bankingcode.org.uk.

2.2.1 Banking and Business Banking Codes 2005

Since 1992, financial services organisations in the UK have subscribed to a **Banking Code** for personal customers. Since 31 March 2002, there has also been a **Business Banking Code**, which offers the same protection to business customers with a turnover of up to £1m per annum. The most recent editions came into force on 1 March 2005.

The Codes cover current accounts including basic bank accounts, savings accounts, including mini-cash and tax-exempt special savings account individual savings accounts (TESSA ISAs); personal loans and overdrafts, card products and payment services, including foreign exchange services.

The Current Banking Codes contain standards that cover:

◆ choosing products and services;

◆ running/conducting accounts;

◆ borrowing money;

◆ interest rates, charges and terms and conditions, and how any changes to these will be communicated;

- cards and personal identification numbers (PINs);

- protecting the account and personal information;

- moving or closing accounts;

- dealing with financial difficulties;

- complaints.

The key commitments and responsibilities set out by the financial services organisations under the Banking Codes are indicated below.

Our key commitments to you
We promise that we will act fairly and reasonably in all our dealings with you by meeting all the commitments and standards in this Code.
The key commitments are shown below.

- We will make sure that our advertising and promotional literature is clear and not misleading and that you are given clear information about our products and services.

- When you have chosen an account or service we will give you clear information about how it works, the terms and conditions and the interest rates which apply to it.

- We will help you use your account or service by sending you regular statements (where appropriate) and we will keep you informed about changes to the interest rates, charges or terms and conditions.

- We will deal quickly and sympathetically with things that go wrong and consider all cases of financial difficulty sympathetically and positively.

- We will treat all your personal information as private and confidential, and operate secure and reliable banking and payment systems.

- We will publicise this Code, have copies available and make sure that our staff are trained to put it into practice.

Source: The Banking Code Standards Board (2005).

2.2.2 The Banking Code Standards Board (BCSB)

The **Banking Code Standards Board (BCSB)** was set up in 1999 as an independent organisation. Its main roles are to:

- assist banks, building societies and other banking service providers in interpreting the Codes;

- monitor and enforce the Codes;

- take disciplinary action in cases in which there are material breaches of the Codes;

- advocate changes when the Codes are revised;

- promote awareness of the Codes.

2.3　The Financial Ombudsman Service (FOS)

Ombudsmen are set up as an independent and impartial means of resolving certain disputes outside the courts. Ombudsmen are complaint-handling bodies; complainants who make use of ombudsmen continue to retain the right of recourse to the courts of law if necessary. The British and Irish Ombudsman Association (BIOA) has as its members various ombudsmen from the UK (England, Wales, Scotland and Northern Ireland), the Republic of Ireland, the Channel Islands, the Isle of Man and the UK's overseas territories. The most relevant for the UK lender is the Financial Ombudsman Service.

The Financial Ombudsman Service was established by Parliament to resolve disputes between financial services providers and their customers fairly, reasonably, quickly and informally. The service is independent and impartial, and is free to consumers. Each year, approximately 500,000 enquiries are dealt with and 100,000 disputes settled. On average, most disputes are settled within six to nine months.

Consumers are not compelled to accept any decision made by the FOS and are free to go to court instead. If they accept an ombudsman's decision, however, it is binding both on them and on the financial services provider.

The FOS looks into complaints about most financial matters, including:

◆ banking;

◆ insurance;

◆ mortgages;

◆ pensions;

◆ savings and investments;

◆ credit cards and store cards;

◆ loans and credit;

◆ hire purchase and pawnbroking;

◆ financial advice;

◆ stocks, shares, unit trusts and bonds.

2.4　Customer rights and complaint procedures

The **lender** has a duty to:

◆ provide a formal and free complaint handling service;

◆ acknowledge any complaint promptly and to provide information about the complaint-handling services;

◆ investigate a complaint, and give a clear and fair answer within eight weeks.

A **customer** has a right to:

♦ be clearly informed about a firm's complaint handling service;

♦ make a complaint if it is thought that there are valid grounds for doing so;

♦ if not satisfied with the firm's response:

– take the complaint to an independent complaints scheme, such as the FOS; or

– take the case to court.

Some of the areas in which a customer might have a right of redress are outlined in the FSA's MoneyMadeClear™ guide on making complaints (FSA, 2007a):

♦ unexpected or excessive charges;

♦ losing money because of the firm's slow administration;

♦ dispute over who is at fault if money is stolen from an account;

♦ incorrect or misleading information about a product;

♦ a firm's failure to adequately warn you about the risks of a product, or to advise properly on its suitability for you; or

♦ a firm's failure to draw attention to a particularly strict condition in the contract;

♦ a firm's failure to carry out your instructions;

♦ you haven't been given adequate notice about changes to a contract.

Source: FSA, 2007a

2.5   Treating customers fairly

The FSA envisages that a move to **more principles based regulation (MPBR)** will offer financial services organisations greater flexibility to determine for themselves how to deliver fair treatment to their customers in a way that suits their business. As against the rigidity of a prescriptive rule-based approach, the flexibility of the principles-based approach is expected to facilitate greater competition and innovation, which, in turn, would promote more efficient markets that would better enable consumers to achieve fair treatment.

2.5.1   The Treating Customers Fairly (TCF) initiative

The initiative of **Treating Customers Fairly (TCF)** is identified as central to the delivery of the FSA's retail regulatory agenda as well as being a key part of its move to principles-based regulation.

Firms have an obligation to act fairly under FSMA 2000, through the FSA's **Principles for Businesses**, which underpin the work that it is doing with firms as part of the TCF initiative.

- Principle 6 requires a firm to 'pay due regard to the interests of its customers and treat them fairly'.

- Principle 7 requires a firm to 'pay due regard to the information needs of its customers and communicate information to them in a way which is clear, fair and not misleading'.

TCF is described as a cultural issue as the right organisational culture must be established in order to ensure fair outcomes for consumers. Through the TCF initiative the FSA aims to deliver the following six improved outcomes for retail consumers (FSA, 2007b).

- **Outcome 1:** Consumers can be confident that they are dealing with firms where the fair treatment of customers is central to the corporate culture.

- **Outcome 2:** Products and services marketed and sold in the retail market are designed to meet the needs of identified consumer groups and are targeted accordingly.

- **Outcome 3:** Consumers are provided with clear information and are kept appropriately informed before, during and after the point of sale.

- **Outcome 4:** Where consumers receive advice, the advice is suitable and takes account of their circumstances.

- **Outcome 5:** Consumers are provided with products that perform as firms have led them to expect, and the associated service is both of an acceptable standard and as they have been led to expect.

- **Outcome 6:** consumers do not face unreasonable post-sale barriers imposed by firms to change product, switch provider, submit a claim or make a complaint.

The FSA has set various deadlines in relation to the implementation of TCF programmes. By the end of March 2008, firms are expected to have appropriate measures in place to test whether they are treating their customers fairly and, by the end of December 2008, all firms are expected to be able to demonstrate that they are consistently treating their customers fairly.

2.5.2 Unfair Contract Terms Act 1977

Section 11(1) of the Unfair Contract Terms Act 1977 requires that a contractual term needs to pass the reasonableness test: '...the term shall have been a fair and reasonable one to be included having regard to the circumstances which were, or ought reasonably to have been, known to or in the contemplation of the parties when the contract was made'. An unfair contract term is defined in reg 5(1) of the Unfair Terms in Consumer Contracts Regulations 1999, SI 1999/2083) as: 'A contractual term which has not been individually negotiated shall be regarded as unfair if, contrary to the requirement of good faith, it causes a significant imbalance in the parties' rights and obligations arising under the contract, to the detriment of the consumer'.

As a qualifying body under these Regulations, the FSA is empowered to challenge a firm in court about its use of any terms deemed to be unfair.

It is important that lenders keep abreast of legal and regulatory developments that might impact upon their lending function. Membership of trade bodies such as the British Bankers' Association (BBA) and the Association of British Insurers (ABI), with the attendant benefits of networking and information flows, will help lenders to keep up to date and will also inform policy that, in turn, will impact upon the legal and regulatory framework.

Conclusion

In order to be effective, the lending function needs to be regulated by the lending organisations themselves as well as by independent authorities. It is necessary to understand the regulatory environment in order to be able to develop effective lending policies and practices.

The UK has adopted a tripartite system of regulation, involving the Treasury, the Bank of England and the Financial Services Authority.

Relevant law needs to be constantly kept in view by those who exercise the lending function. Some of the more important pieces of legislation in the UK include the Financial Services and Markets Act 2000 (FSMA), the Consumer Credit Acts 1974 and 2006, the Insolvency Acts 1986, 1994 and 2000, the Enterprise Act 2002, the Data Protection Act 1998, the Freedom of Information Act 2000 and the Unfair Contract Terms Act 1977.

In 1988 the Basel Committee on Banking Supervision of the Bank for International Settlements proposed a set of minimal capital requirements for banks, and these became law in the UK and most other G-10 countries in 1992. Basel II is the second of the Basel Accords, and the revised comprehensive framework (Basel, 2006) is designed to promote the adoption of stronger risk management practices by the banking industry.

Banking Codes are voluntary, and attempt to set minimum standards for the way in which banks and other financial services providers should treat their customers. Financial services organisations in the UK subscribe to a Banking Code for certain personal and business customers. The most recent editions are The Banking and Business Banking Codes 2005. The Banking Code Standards Board (BCSB) was set up in 1999 as an independent organisation to assist banks, building societies and other banking service providers in interpreting, monitoring and enforcing the Codes. The Financial Ombudsman Service was established by Parliament to resolve disputes between financial services providers and their customers fairly, reasonably, quickly and informally.

The lender has a duty to provide a formal and free complaint handling service to customers. The initiative of treating customers fairly (TCF) has been identified as central to the delivery of the FSA's retail regulatory agenda as well as being a key part of its move to principles-based regulation.

Further reading

Barth, J. R., Caprio, G. and Levine, R. (2007) *Rethinking Bank Regulation: Till Angels Govern*, Cambridge: Cambridge University Press.

Matthews, K., Murinde, V. and Zhaoc, T. (2007) 'Competitive conditions among the major British banks', *Journal of Banking & Finance*, **31**, 2025–42.

Topic 2
Review questions and activities

The following review questions and activities are designed to increase your understanding of the material you have just studied.

◆ The **review questions** are designed so that you can check your understanding of this topic.

◆ Completion of the **activities** will give you further opportunity to research and understand, in more depth, the themes running through this topic.

The answers to the questions and case study are provided at the end of these learning materials. Please note that the activities are open-ended and therefore a suitable 'answer' may not always be provided.

Review questions

[?]

1. Identify the three authorities that form part of the tripartite system of regulation in the UK.

2. Identify some of the important statutes that might be relevant to the lender in the UK.

3. Identify some of the areas covered by the Banking Codes.

4. What is the role of the Financial Ombudsman Service (FOS)?

5. What is the Treating Customers Fairly (TCF) initiative?

Activities

Activity 1

> Visit the UK statute law database at www.statutelaw.gov.uk
>
> Browse through the various statutes that have been covered in this section.

Activity 2

> Visit the following websites and conduct searches for 'lending', 'credit' and similar key words.
>
> ◆ The Financial Services Authority: www.fsa.gov.uk
>
> ◆ The Banking Code Standards Board: www.bankingcode.org.uk
>
> ◆ The Information Commissioner's Office: www.ico.gov.uk
>
> ◆ The Financial Ombudsman Service: www.financial-ombudsman.org.uk
>
> ◆ The British and Irish Ombudsman Association: http://www.bioa.org.uk/
>
> ◆ The Office of Fair Trading: www.oft.gov.uk/
>
> ◆ 10 Downing Street: www.number10.gov.uk

Topic 3
Types of borrower

Learning outcomes

By the end of this topic, students should be able to understand the nature of different types of borrowers.

Learning areas include:

◆ individuals and sole traders;

◆ partnerships;

◆ companies;

◆ clubs and societies;

◆ trusts;

◆ others.

Introduction

The lender needs to bear in mind an important principle: 'Know your customer'. The law requires this in order to combat money laundering and other types of criminal activity. Knowing the borrower also enables a lender to:

◆ safeguard against fraud, recognise suspicious/illegal activity, and protect against reputational and financial risks;

◆ avoid recommending the wrong product to the customer and provide only those lending products that are suitable;

◆ monitor lending activity in an effective manner;

◆ avoid a situation of not being able to recover an advance because the lender was not aware of the legal implications of lending to that particular customer type.

The lender needs to understand not only the nature of the borrower, but also the industry in which they operate, the competition, the location and many other factors.

While a number of hybrid varieties are continually being created, the major types of borrower can be classified under the following heads.

- ◆ **Personal borrowers:**
  - – individuals;
  - – sole traders;
  - – minors.
- ◆ **Partnerships:**
  - – partnerships;
  - – limited partnerships;
  - – limited liability partnerships.
- ◆ **Limited companies:**
  - – public limited companies;
  - – private limited companies;
  - – community interest companies.
- ◆ **Unincorporated associations:**
  - – clubs and societies;
  - – trusts.
- ◆ Others.

3.1   Personal borrowers

Personal borrowers can operate singly or in joint accounts. They can be adults or minors, and they can operate in their own names or as a sole trader in the name of a business.

3.1.1 Individuals

> An **individual** is a person or body of persons not all of whom are corporate bodies and that is not a partnership.

The terms and conditions of loans to an individual are relatively simple. The loan agreement will indicate details such as the amount of the loan, interest payable, repayment terms, details of any collateral security, and any other terms and conditions to which the loan would be subject. The borrower will indicate acceptance of the loan by signing on the duplicate copy of the loan letter and returning it to the lender. Private individuals bear the same rights and responsibilities as sole proprietors.

3.1.2 Sole traders

> Sole proprietorships are unincorporated businesses owned by a single person who has the right to profits and is liable for its debts. A sole trader is a person who is the sole owner of a business, regardless of whether other people are employed to help run the business.

A **sole trader** may adopt a different name for the business. For example, Joe Lee might run Somerset Gardening Services, but the law will not distinguish between the assets of Joe Lee and Somerset Gardening Services.

The sole trader has complete responsibility for all of the debts of the business or bears unlimited liability, unlike a limited company or limited partnership. Some lenders are reluctant to extend credit to a sole trader, because they have a higher rate of bankruptcy.

3.1.3 Minors

> According to the Family Law Reform Act 1969, a person attains full age on reaching the age of 18. Thus a **minor** is a person who is under the age of 18.

While a minor is able to ratify any loans that might have been taken on achieving majority, a minor might be able to repudiate a loan contract, because a minor's debts are not always enforceable, particularly if the loans have not been given for 'necessaries' (*Coutts v Browne-Lecky* [1947]). Lenders will therefore need to be cautious about lending to minors and will usually require the guarantee of an adult in order to safeguard repayment. The Minors' Contracts Act 1987 provides some protection to the lender: s 2(b) states that where a minor's debt is guaranteed by an adult and the contract is repudiated, 'the guarantee shall not for that reason alone be unenforceable against the guarantor'. Lenders are therefore able to rely on the guarantor for the repayment of a debt repudiated by a minor.

Lenders also have remedy in the form of the **doctrine of subrogation** whereby the lender is entitled to 'stand in the shoes' of a third party. A lender who has lent money to pay for a purchase by a minor will be able to stand in the shoes (ie take the place) of the seller of the goods and exercise the rights of the seller.

3.2 Partnerships

> **Partnerships** are associations of two or more persons who have entered into a legal contract by which each agrees to furnish a part of the capital and labour for a business enterprise, and under which each shares a fixed proportion of profits and losses, and they are individually and jointly liable for the debts of the business.

3.2.1 Partnership firms

The Partnership Act 1890 sets out the basic structure of partnership. Some of the characteristics of a partnership firm are summed up as follows.

- Section 1(1) of the Partnership Act 1890 defines a partnership as 'the relation which subsists between persons carrying on a business in common with a view of profit'. The relationship between members of any company is specifically excluded from the definition of partnerships (s 1(2)(a)).

- Any two or more persons can form a partnership.

- Every partner is an agent of the firm for the purpose of the business of the firm and can bind the firm and other partners.

- Every partner in a firm is liable jointly with the other partners for all debts and obligations of the firm incurred while they were a partner.

- Persons who, by words or by conduct, represent themselves, or are 'holding out' as a partner in a firm, is liable as a partner to anyone who has, on the faith of such representation, given credit to the firm.

- All of the partners are entitled to share equally in the capital and profits of the business, and are required to contribute equally towards the losses.

- A partnership is dissolved:

    - if specified, on the expiration of any term;

    - if specified, on the termination of any undertaking;

    - on any partner giving notice to the others of an intention to dissolve the partnership;

    - on bankruptcy or death of any partner;

    - on the occurrence any event that makes it illegal for the business of the firm to be carried on;

    - on the issue of a court decree that a partner is of mentally incapable or of unsound mind;

    - on the retirement of an existing partner or the admission of a new partner.

- In terms of liability to lenders:

    - a person who is admitted as a partner into an existing firm is not liable to the creditors of the firm for anything done before they became a partner;

    - a partner who retires from a firm does not cease to be liable for partnership debts incurred before their retirement.

- The rights and duties of partners may be varied by the express or implied consent of all of the partners.

- The articles of partnership can vary some of the legal provisions.

Lenders need to be aware that the rule in *Clayton's Case* (*Devaynes v Noble* [1816]) will apply when a partnership is dissolved. This records the principle of 'first incurred first discharged', whereby a credit to a customer's account is deemed to discharge the earliest of the debit item on the account. To avoid the operation of the rule, it will be necessary to break the account and to recommence with an account for the new partnership. In *Royal Bank of Scotland v Christie* [1841] a partner mortgaged his personal property to secure the debts of a partnership firm. On his death the firm was overdrawn, but the bank did not rule off the account which continued unbroken. The surviving partners paid amounts into the account that exceeded the debit balance at the deceased partner's death and then withdrew an even larger balance. The court held that the payments into the account after the death of the partner went towards paying off the deceased partner's mortgage.

3.2.2 Limited partnerships

The Limited Partnerships Act 1907 introduced a second form of partnership, in which the liability of one or more of the partners could be limited, while retaining general partners with unlimited liability. Some of the characteristics of a **limited partnership** are summed up below.

◆ A limited partnership consists of one or more persons called **general partners** who are liable for all debts and obligations of the firm, and one or more persons called **limited partners** who contribute to capital or property but who are not liable for the debts or obligations of the firm beyond the amount contributed.

◆ A limited partner cannot:

    – draw out or receive back any part of their contribution;

    – take part in the management of the partnership business;

    – bind the firm.

◆ If a limited partner does take part in the management of the partnership business, they will be liable for all debts and obligations of the firm incurred while they took part in the management as if they were a general partner.

◆ A limited partnership will not be dissolved by the death or bankruptcy of a limited partner, and the mental incapacity of a limited partner will not generally be a ground for dissolution of the partnership by the court.

◆ A corporate body may be a limited partner.

3.2.3 Limited liability partnerships

The **limited liability partnership (LLP)** is a new type of corporate vehicle created by the Limited Liability Partnership (LLP) Act 2000 (the LLP Act). The LLP structure has been adopted by a range of firms in a number of sectors. Most of the large accountancy and legal firms are LLPs, and the form is also used by a number of medical practices and small firms. Some of the characteristics of a LLP are summed up below.

◆ Any two or more persons can form as an LLP. Members have the flexibility of organising their internal structure as in the case of a traditional partnership.

◆ Members are generally taxed in the same way as partners in a partnership.

◆ Unlike a company, the LLP does not have shares or shareholders or directors.

◆ The LLP is registered on the Companies House Register.

◆ Like a company, it is a legal entity separate from its members and therefore enjoys the benefit of limited liability. While the LLP is liable for the full extent of its debts, the liability of the members is limited, except to the extent that the members agree otherwise.

♦ Subsequent regulations broadly apply large parts of the Insolvency Act 1986 and the Companies Act 2006 to the LLP. It is subject to similar accounting and disclosure provisions.

3.3 Companies

> **Companies**, or **corporations**, are separate legal entities formed for the purpose of undertaking a business (*Salomon v Salomon and Co Ltd* [1897]). Companies are owned by shareholders, who have the right to participate in the profits, through dividends and/or the appreciation of stock, but are not personally liable for the company's debts. The day-to-day management of companies are undertaken by directors appointed by the shareholders. Companies can be private or public. A **public corporation** is one in which anyone can buy shares of stock, which may be traded on a stock exchange. A **private corporation** is one in which the sale of stock may be limited to stipulated persons, such as members of the principal stockholder's family.

Section 1(1) of the Companies Act 2006 defines a company as 'a company that is formed and registered under this Act'. The Companies Act 2006, thought to be the longest Act ever to have been passed by Parliament and which will apply to all limited companies, repeals and restates almost all of the current Companies Acts, which it will largely replace. The new Companies Act 2006, which will affect directors, auditors, shareholders and company secretaries of private and public companies, will come into force by October 2008. However, some provisions have taken effect on 31 December 2006 and January 2007; companies are now required to disclose their registered name and number on company websites and order forms, and they are now allowed to communicate electronically with shareholders and others.

Companies can be limited or unlimited, public or private.

Prior to the commencecment of the Companies Act 2006, companies will have had the following documentation.

♦ A **memorandum of association**, which regulates the affairs of the company: this states the company name, the location of the registered office, the objects of the company and its liability.

♦ **articles of association**, which regulate the actions of the directors.

♦ A **trading certificate or certificate to commence business**: any debts incurred before this certificate is issued will be deemed to be pre-incorporation debts and the company may not be liable, as it had not yet assumed a legal identity when the debts were incurred.

The objects clause that appears in the memorandum of association was intended to exclude the possibility of a company acting ***ultra vires***, that is, beyond its proper powers. Ultra vires actions once carried risks for lenders, depriving them of enforceable security and the possibility of recovering their money if the company became insolvent. It was subsequently held, however, that, providing that a third party such as a bank lender acted in good faith, it was not to be prejudiced by any deficiency in a company's constitution.

Under the Companies Act 2006 the position will become even simpler: with effect from October 2008, the objects clause will be removed from the memorandum, along with most of the rest of the document. The memorandum will be reduced to a simple statement that the initial subscribers wish to form a company and agree to become members and take at least one share each. Only if the articles contain some specific restriction will the company be limited in its actions. For example, a company that is a charity, will be limited to objects that are of a charitable nature.

In general, the effect of the Act will be to take away the need to be concerned about whether the borrowing company has the right objects or powers in its constitution.

If, in a winding-up, it appears that any business has been carried on with the intent of defrauding creditors or for any other fraudulent reason, the court may declare that any 'knowing parties' are guilty of **fraudulent trading** and personally liable to make such contributions as the court thinks proper. In *Re William C Leitch Bros Ltd* [1933] it was held to be fraudulent to continue to trade when directors knew that there was no reasonable prospect of paying debts. In 2007, Michael Bright, who had been the chief executive of Independent Insurance when it collapsed dramatically in 2001, was handed down the maximum penalty of ten years' imprisonment for fraudulent trading. **Wrongful trading** takes place when the directors know, or ought to have known, that there is no reasonable prospect that the company would avoid insolvent liquidation. In *Re Produce Marketing Consortium Ltd* [1989] it was held that reasonable standard of skill expected of a director will vary depending upon the size of the company.

Fraudulent and wrongful trading can lead to a person's disqualification from being a director.

3.3.1 Limited or unlimited companies

A company is a **limited company** if the liability of its members is limited by its constitution. It may be limited by shares or limited by guarantee.

If their liability is limited to the amount, if any, unpaid on the shares held by them, the company is **limited by shares**.

If their liability is limited to such amount as the members undertake to contribute to the assets of the company in the event of its being wound up, the company is **limited by guarantee**.

If there is no limit on the liability of its members, the company is an **unlimited company**.

3.3.2 Public and private companies

> The initials 'plc' after a UK company name indicate that it is a **public limited company**, a type of limited company in which shares may be offered for sale to the public.

A public company is a company:

♦ limited by shares or limited by guarantee and having share capital;

♦ the certificate of incorporation of which states that it is a public company;

♦ in relation to which the requirements of the Companies Acts as to registration or re-registration as a public company have been complied with.

A public company *must not do business or exercise any borrowing powers* unless:

♦ the registrar has issued it with a 'trading certificate';

♦ the nominal value of the company's allotted share capital is not less than the authorised minimum;

♦ at least one quarter of the nominal value of the share capital has been paid up.

Thus a lender must, on no account lend money to a public company before it has been issued with a trading certificate or a certificate to commence business.

> A **private company** is any company that is not a public company. The appearance of 'Ltd' after a UK company name indicates that it is a **private limited company**.

3.3.3 Community interest companies

A **community interest company (CIC)** is a company that is:

♦ limited by shares or by guarantee and, not having share capital, may be formed as, or may become a community interest company;

♦ limited by guarantee and, having share capital, may become a community interest company.

Examples of CICs (as taken from http://www.cicregulator.gov.uk/guidance.shtml on 7.3.2008), include:

♦ companies formed to provide their members with a service that meets a pressing social need, or to provide jobs to disadvantage people who would otherwise be unlikely to find employment, could satisfy the test because its activities would benefit the wider community as well as its members or employees;

♦ a sports club for employees of a business may only satisfy the test if it provides a wider community benefit, for example, by making its facilities available to the local community or providing training facilities not otherwise available in the area;

◆ a company formed by the employees of a business solely for their own profit, such as a bulk purchasing discount scheme, would not satisfy the test. If, however, teh sports club ran a purchasing scheme as an incidental activity that contributed to the community objectives of the club, this may not affect its eligibility to be a CIC.

3.4   Unincorporated associations

3.4.1 Clubs and societies

> A **club**, or **society**, is a group of people organised for a common purpose, distinguished by mutual interests and generally arranging to meet at regular intervals, eg a book club, a garden club, a badminton club.

The club or society will generally:

◆ identify the objectives of the group;

◆ set out the rules of the club or society in a governing document;

◆ designate office-bearers who are authorised to sign on its behalf;

◆ record minutes of committee meetings;

◆ have a chairperson, secretary and treasurer: the treasurer will be responsible for the organisation's finances, including finding a bank account;

◆ appoint an auditor or independent examiner to check the accounts.

Any decision to have a bank account or to borrow will be recorded in the form of a resolution at a committee meeting.

A club or society is defined by the Charities Commission as a means by which people share a common interest and create a formal structure through which they can pursue it. Section 3(1) of the Charities Act 2006 states that it 'must be for the public benefit if it is to be a charitable purpose'. The Charity Commission regulates charities of all sizes and forms.

In order to gain charitable status, the group has to fulfill one of the following functions:

◆ providing relief for the poor, handicapped and/or disabled;

◆ assisting the advancement of education;

◆ furthering the promotion of religion;

◆ making other beneficial contributions to the community.

From 23 April 2007, a charity only has to be registered if its annual income is over £5,000.

3.4.2 Trusts

A **trustee** is a person who holds legal title to an asset for the benefit of another. A **trust** is a fiduciary relationship in which one party, known as a **creator**, **grantor**, **donor** or **trustor**, gives another party, the trustee, the right to hold title to assets for the benefit of a third party, who will be the beneficiary of the trust.

Power to permit trustees to borrow money and/or charge trust property can be found:

◆ in the governing document;

◆ in the Trusts of Land and Appointment of Trustees Act 1996;

◆ in the Trustee Act 2000;

◆ by implication.

Where trustees do not have the power to borrow and/or to charge property, they can confer a suitable power on the charity by using the power of amendment for unincorporated charities (under s 74D of the Charities Act 1993, as inserted by the Charities Act 2006) or the power of amendment available to companies under the Companies Acts. In the unlikely event that the governing document specifically precludes borrowing, a scheme will be required to authorise it. The exercise of any power of borrowing and/or charging property must be strictly in accordance with the terms of the power.

3.4.3 Others

A country can be a borrower. A sovereign borrower might be the government itself or a ministry of the government.

An understanding of the various types of borrower will enable the lender to be more effective in exercising the lending function.

Conclusion

The lender needs to bear in mind an important principle: 'know your customer'. Knowing the borrower enables a lender to safeguard against fraud, recognise suspicious or illegal activity and protect against reputational and financial risks.

The major types of borrowers can be classified as partnerships, limited companies, unincorporated associations and others.

Personal borrowers can operate singly or in joint accounts; they can be majors or minors; they can operate in their own names or as a sole trader in the name of a business.

Partnerships are associations of two or more persons who have entered into a legal contract by which each agrees to provide a part of the capital and labour for a business enterprise. The Partnership Act 1890 sets out the basic structure of partnership, and defines a partnership as 'relation which subsists between persons carrying on a business in common with a view of profit'. The Limited Partnerships

Act 1907 introduced a second form of partnership, in which the liability of one or more of the partners could be limited, while retaining general partners with unlimited liability. The Limited Liability Partnership is a new type of corporate vehicle created by the Limited Liability Partnership Act 2000 (the LLP Act).

Companies (or corporations) are separate legal entities formed for the purpose of undertaking a business. Companies are owned by shareholders who have the right to participate in the profits, through dividends and/or the appreciation of stock, but are not personally liable for the company's debts. Companies are usually public limited companies (plc) or private limited companies (Ltd). A company limited by shares or a company limited by guarantee may be formed as or become a community interest company.

A club or society is a group of people organised for a common purpose, distinguished by mutual interests, and generally arrange to meet at regular intervals. A trust is a fiduciary relationship in which one party, known as a creator, grantor, donor, or trustor, gives another party, the trustee, the right to hold title to assets for the benefit of a third party, who will be the beneficiary of the trust.

A country can be a borrower; a government itself or a ministry in the government can be a borrower. Thus there can be a variety of types of borrower. An understanding of the various types of borrowers will enable the lender to be more effective in exercising the lending function.

Further reading

ifs *KnowledgeBank* Subject Gateway, (2005) *'Know your customer'*.

The Times, 100 'Types of businesses'.

Topic 3

Review questions and activities

The following review questions and activities are designed to increase your understanding of the material you have just studied.

◆ The **review questions** are designed so that you can check your understanding of this topic.

◆ Completion of the **activities** will give you further opportunity to research and understand, in more depth, the themes running through this topic.

The answers to the questions and case study are provided at the end of these learning materials. Please note that the activities are open-ended and therefore a suitable 'answer' may not always be provided.

Review questions

?

1. Why is it important to understand the nature of the borrower?

2. What is the risk of lending to a minor?

3. Distinguish between 'partnerships', 'limited partnerships' and 'limited liability partnerships'.

4. Distinguish between 'public limited companies' and 'private limited companies'.

5. Are trusts entitled to borrow money?

Activities

Activity 1

Look at 'the 'London Share Services' section of the *Financial Times*. Identify the various industry classifications of public limited companies. Select a company that interests you and telephone the cityline number and request a copy of the company's financial statements.

Go through the statements when you are receive them. How might a lender use the information available in the documents?

Activity 2

Visit the following websites and identify the nature of companies and how they differ from unincorporated clubs and societies:

www.companieshouse.gov.uk/

www.charity-commission.gov.uk/index.asp

Topic 4
The purposes of financing

Learning outcomes

By the end of this topic, students should be able to understand particular types of lending requirement, and the types of finance that can be made available to meet differing customer needs.

Learning areas include:

◆ forms of consumer finance, including bridging loans and house purchase;

◆ working capital;

◆ new ventures;

◆ business expansion;

◆ purchase of fixed assets.

Introduction

Lending can be extended for a variety of reasons. Some of the purposes of lending are indicated in Figure 4.1.

Figure 4.1 The purposes of financing

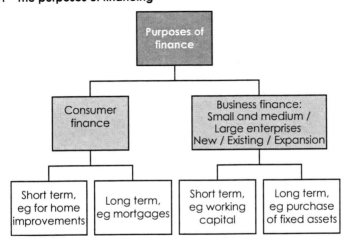

A period of a year or less is generally considered to be short term, while periods in excess of a year are classified as long term.

4.1   Consumer finance

In general, **consumer finance** means finance that is extended to consumers.

Specifically, consumer finance refers to finance extended to personal consumers as opposed to business customers. Consumer finance can be extended for a short term, eg loans for home improvements, cars, electrical and white goods purchase, or for a long term, eg mortgages for house purchases. Consumer finance can be made available for a range of purposes. Some of these purposes are examined in section 4.1.1 and section 4.1.3. Personal loans are frequently granted on the ability of the borrower to repay and without a specific purpose appearing in the facility letter.

4.1.1   Bridging loans

A **bridging loan** serves to bridge a gap in the form of interim financing until the way is cleared for longer term financing to be obtained.

A bridging loan is usually taken out to meet a temporary cash shortfall that may arise when buying a property or business. A bridging loan will usually involve lending a large sum of money over a short period (generally not more than six months) at higher interest rates to compensate for the higher risk, as the borrower might effectively have to service two or more loans at the same time.

The loan amount will depend upon the valuation of available security and will be given against the security of equity available in the assets being financed. The **loan to value (LTV) ratio** will generally be lower than that for standard mortgages, typically not more than 65-70%.

Income from the sale of a property will usually form the principal source of repayment of the interim bridging loan.

There are two major types of bridging loan.

♦ **Closed bridging**, where the loan is for a defined period – offered when the date of availability of funds for closing the loan is known in advance, eg when the date of completion of sale of the old home has been fixed.

♦ **Open bridging**, where the loan is open-ended and the closure date is not known. This type of loan will be charged a higher rate of interest to compensate for the higher risk.

Some of the purposes for offering bridging finance might be to:

◆ bridge the gap between the purchase of a new home and the sale of the old home – that is to buy a second property before the first property has been sold;

◆ buy a property at auction, in respect of the required 10% deposit;

◆ buy a home needing renovation before occupation, pending subsequent receipt of mortgage funds.

Bridging loans are also used in venture capital and corporate finance to finance interim needs, eg between successive financings, or immediately prior to an initial public offering.

4.1.1.1 Solicitors undertakings

Security for bridging loans is usually provided by an undertaking from a solicitor to forward to the lender either the proceeds from the sale of the old property or the funds from the mortgage lender following completion of the conditions under which the mortgage was offered (such as the completion of remedial work for which the bridging loan was advanced).

4.1.2 Probate loans

When a person dies their financial estate is assessed as to its overall value. If the estate is being left entirely to a surviving spouse there will be no tax to pay on any level. However, if it is not left to a spouse, and it exceeds the inheritance tax threshold (set at £300,000 for 2007/08), then inheritance tax will be due (at a rate of 40% in 2008). Readers should ensure that they are aware of the current threshold and tax rate.

Under current English law, the inheritance tax must be paid to HM Revenue & Customs (HMRC) before any distribution to the beneficiaries. This can often cause a short-term liquidity problem.

Consider the following situation. A person dies leaving the following assets:

	£
House	350,000
Stocks and shares	75,000
Gilts	100,000
Bank account	15,000
Total estate	**540,000**
IHT threshold	300,000
Taxable estate	240,000
Tax due	**96,000**

It is the responsibility of the executor to pay this £96,000 to HMRC before payment to the beneficiaries. The chances are that they will not have the cash available and you cannot sell part of the assets to pay the bill. The solution is a probate loan.

There are two possible sources for this facility:

♦ the executor's banker – they will know you but will take convincing of the value of the estate;

♦ the deceased's banker – they will likely know the value of the estate but probably not you.

Despite the disadvantages inherent in both choices, you will almost certainly be granted the facility. The main consideration in this lending decision is the type of loan itself, although the structure of the estate is also relevant. In this simple example the facility will be very short term. As soon as the tax liability has been discharged you will be able to effect repayment from the sale of shares or gilts.

The situation would be made more complex if the estate were made up entirely of property. Selling the house could take longer, or the beneficiaries might wish to live in the house. In this case they would need to raise a mortgage loan on the property to repay the probate loan. Before granting a probate loan, you will want sight of the will, or letters of administration (in the case of someone dying intestate).

4.1.3 Mortgages

A **mortgage** is a legal agreement conveying conditional ownership of assets as security for a loan. In colloquial terms, it refers to a loan secured by a mortgage of fixed assets. In banking terms, it refers to the security provided to cover either a loan or an overdraft.

The person offering the mortgage is the **mortgagor** and the institution lending money against the security of the mortgage is the **mortgagee**. Mortgages are generally extended to owners of residential property as well as to leaseholders with lease periods that have at least 70 or 80 years remaining to run. Mortgage payments are generally required to be made at monthly intervals.

There are various types of mortgage.

♦ A **repayment mortgage** is one that is repaid by a regular monthly payment, which includes interest on the capital plus an element of capital repayment.

♦ An **interest-only mortgage** or **endowment mortgage** is one under which only interest is paid during the life of the loan, the principal being repaid in one lump sum from the proceeds of a separate investment in an endowment fund or an ISA or a similar investment vehicle.

♦ Under a **shared appreciation mortgage (SAM)**, the lender acquires a stake in any increases in property value. Lenders are reported to have been able to achieve an effective interest rate of up to 70% in times of rising house prices. Morgan Stanley's 'Flexishare mortgage' is a shared equity mortgage available at up to seven times income, where the lender can share in the profits and losses at up to a maximum of 35%.

♦ **Consolidation loans** usually convert a number of unsecured loans into one loan secured by residential property.

The lender needs to be able to assess the suitability of a mortgage to the needs of the client. A comparison of repayment and endowment mortgages is given below.

◆ **Investment risk** – many homeowners who took out endowment mortgages were faced with unexpected financial problems when the average growth rate of the endowment fund was not sufficient to cover the mortgage capital.

◆ **The amount of interest paid** – the outstanding balance of an endowment mortgage does not decrease over time and therefore more interest is paid over the life of an endowment mortgage than over the life of a repayment mortgage.

◆ **The impact of interest rate risk** – an increase in interest rate would normally cause a greater change in the interest outgoings under an endowment mortgage, while simultaneously causing downward pressure on the value of the investment portfolio.

◆ **Tax implications** – because interest can be set off as expenses in respect of buy-to-let or business mortgages the tax relief will be higher for an endowment mortgage in these cases.

◆ **Charges** – the additional tax relief that an endowment mortgage might enjoy is, however, usually offset by a high premium or the substantial commissionspaid to financial advisers and investment companies for securing this business, although competition has been driving down the differential between mortgages for residential occupation and buy-to-let mortgages.

◆ **Life insurance** – an endowment mortgage has built-in life insurance, whereas with a repayment mortgage, separate life insurance may need to be taken out.

> A **second mortgage** is a type of subordinate mortgage made while an original mortgage is still in existence.

In the event of default, the original mortgage will have priority; the proceeds from the liquidation of the property will be first applied towards the first mortgage. Any remaining proceeds will then be applied to the second mortgage. In bank lending, a second mortgage (or subsequently third, fourth, etc) is any charge over land that ranks after a first charge, and which captures the remaining equity in the property.

Purposes of such borrowing may include:

◆ the purchase of a second home or of a buy-to-let property;

◆ home improvements;

◆ funding a child's education;

◆ purchasing a new vehicle;

◆ consolidating debt and paying off other sources of outstanding debt, which may carry higher interest rates;

◆ overdraft facilities.

4.2 Business finance

> **Business finance** is finance offered by lenders to businesses (as opposed to persons). Businesses can be either small and medium enterprises (SMEs) or large enterprises.

Lending to businesses can be structured depending upon the requirements of the borrower and can vary depending upon:

♦ **currency requirements**, eg domestic or foreign;

♦ **time periods**, eg short term or long term;

♦ **interest rate requirements**, eg variable or fixed;

♦ **repayment terms**: can vary depending on the nature and purpose of the borrowing, seasonal trends and the nature of the business.

4.2.1 New ventures

Lending to new ventures involves a high level of risk in comparison with lending to well-established businesses. New ventures face an uncertain future, carry a higher risk of failure and have limited borrowing options.

Finance can take the form of:

♦ loans and overdrafts;

♦ supplier credit;

♦ venture capital.

While creditors might focus more on past history for extending loans, venture capitalists (which might include banks and bank subsidiaries) might be more interested in future potential and will usually take a stake in the business in the form of equity capital.

> **Venture capital** is capital provided to new start-up business ventures and for business expansion, and has become synonymous with risk capital.

Venture capital has a number of distinctive features.

♦ Venture capital is extended by a range of lenders:

– wealthy individuals sometimes known as 'business angels';

– private equity firms;

– banks, subsidiaries of banks and other financial institutions that pool such investments.

♦ Venture capitalists may offer a mix of debt capital and share capital, thereby acquiring a proportion of the equity.

♦ In addition to finance, venture capitalists will also be providing managerial and technical support for the venture and will acquire a say in company decisions.

♦ Due to the highly speculative nature of their investments, venture capitalists expect a high rate of return. In addition, they often wish to obtain this return over a relatively short period of time, usually within three to seven years.

4.2.2 The expansion of existing business

Lenders will also be approached for finance for the purpose of funding the expansion of existing businesses. Expansion allows a business to meet the demands of a larger customer base, to increase sales volume and to increase profits, providing a greater return to the entrepreneurs.

Expansion can be required for a number of reasons:

◆ targeting new market segments;

◆ diversifying into new products and services;

◆ opening new branches or locations, both domestically and internationally;

◆ starting new distribution methods, such as the telephone and the Internet.

An existing business that plans to expand will have more borrowing options than a new venture, because a business that has been around for some time will have had the opportunity to build up a good financial track record, credit history and reputation. Moreover, the business might have been able to plough its own profits back into the business and may also be in a better position to command forms of finance such as invoice discounting and factoring. Lenders will be more willing to lend to an existing, well-established business than they will to a new venture with an uncertain future.

4.2.3 Working capital requirements

> **Working capital** is an accounting term describing the difference between current assets and current liabilities. As such it will be examined in Topic 6.
>
> Working capital is also the term used by bankers to describe the shortfall of cash available to enable a business to meet its debts, as they fall due.

Cash is generated from either:

◆ sale of stock (or inventory);

◆ collection of debtors (or receivables).

From cash generated, businesses have to pay, among others:

◆ trade creditors;

◆ tax and VAT payments;

◆ loan and other finance payments;

◆ wages and salaries.

Inventory and receivables may not be readily converted to cash to meet payments as they fall due and this cash shortfall is usually met by overdraft facilities.

Alternative methods of managing working capital requirements might include:

◆ reducing inventory (both in amount and time held);

◆ improving production cycle times;

- ◆ collecting debts more efficiently;
- ◆ reducing time allowed to debtors;
- ◆ negotiating increased time from creditors.

These methods often require time to implement and short term borrowing is often the most readily available solution.

Forecasting for working capital requirements is an important part of business management and lenders will need to ensue that such cash budgets (known by lenders and cash flow forecasts):

- ◆ predict expected inflows and outflows of cash;
- ◆ ascertain when possible cash surpluses or shortages might occur, especially in industries with seasonal peaks and troughs;
- ◆ plan ahead;
- ◆ arrange lending/borrowing;
- ◆ to forecast future sales, and the amount and timing of cash receipts;
- ◆ prepare a number of budgets for different eventualities, eg a more optimistic forecast, a more probable forecast or the worst possible forecast.

Lenders of short-term funds will like to see steady growth potential and reliable projected cash flows, demonstrating the ability to repay the borrowing commitments. Even a small change in a company's working capital, however, can make a significant impact on cash flows. The effective management of working capital plays a vital role in providing both cash flow and finance for the increased holding of stock that might be needed for sales growth. A supply chain manager may have a primary goal of ensuring against shortage of stocks of raw materials, but carrying excess inventory levels will lead to higher costs and adversely impact profitability. Working capital management influences both the risks and expected returns of a business: too much working capital will mean reduced profitability while too little will involve an increased risk of disruption to the production processes. This risk–return trade-off underscores the importance of forecasting for working capital requirements. For the lender, the available collateral security will usually be in the form of current assets such as stock and debtors, and therefore the rate of interest will be higher for operating loans reflecting this relatively weaker security position.

Some of the forms in which short-term finance can be extended are:

- ◆ overdrafts;
- ◆ short-term loans;
- ◆ trade and expense credit;
- ◆ short-term leasing and instalment credit;
- ◆ factoring and invoice discounting.

Some of these forms will be considered in detail in Topic 5.

4.2.4 Requirements for purchasing fixed assets

> A **fixed asset** may be defined as any tangible asset that is expected to have a useful life of more than one year and is purchased for use in the business, rather than for resale for profit.

Unlike short-term working capital requirements that need to be financed over periods of less than one year, the purchase of an asset that can be used for a number of years will require lending over a longer period.

Longer-term lending may be required for financing:

◆ the purchase of fixed assets or large capital equipment;

◆ large-scale construction and other projects;

◆ the expansion of facilities or infrastructure or production capacity;

◆ a change in company control or an acquisition.

4.2.5 Short-term or long-term lending?

Lenders need to exercise their discretion as to whether a particular purpose warrants short-term or long-term finance. Traditionally, short-term lending has been considered appropriate for short-term requirements, such as working capital needs by way of overdraft, while long-term loans have been extended for long-term requirements, such as the purchase of fixed assets. But borrower requirements do not always fall into neat categories. For example, some asset requirements might fluctuate with seasonal variations.

Short-term finance is usually cheaper for the borrower than long-term finance, as the probability of things going wrong in the short term is lower and the lender is able to link lending prices more closely to the cost of borrowing. Short-term finance might be more risky, however, because renewal might not be possible when required and the cost of borrowing might rise in the short term. Thus, for the borrower, there is a trade off between the relative cheapness and the risk of short-term debt.

Conclusion

Finance can be made available for a range of purposes. Consumer finance generally means finance that is extended to personal consumers, while business finance is extended to businesses. Businesses can be either small and medium enterprises (SMEs) or large enterprises.

Both consumer finance and business finance can be extended for a short term or long term. A period of a year or less is generally considered to be short term, while periods in excess of a year are classified as long term. Consumer finance can be short term, eg loans for home improvements, or long term, eg mortgages for house purchases.

Business finance will include both lending to new ventures as well as to established businesses. An existing business that plans to expand will have more borrowing options than a new venture, as a business that has been around for some time would have had the opportunity of building up a good financial track record and credit history and reputation.

Traditionally, short-term lending has been considered appropriate for short-term requirements such as working capital needs, while long-term loans have been extended for long-term requirements such as the purchase of fixed assets.

Conclusions as to the ideal lending package are difficult to arrive at. Much depends on the risk–return trade-off for individual borrowers. The general rule of thumb has been that long-term assets should be financed by long-term funds and short-term assets by short-term funds, and that lending should match with the duration of the asset being financed. However many lenders break this rule with great success.

Further reading

Financial Services Authority (2007) *Loans made clear.*

ACCA (2003) *Selecting sources of finance for business.*

Terry, B. (2000), *The International Handbook of Corporate Finance* [ebook] Chicago: New York AMACOM Books. Chapter 2: Principles of Lending – Part II: Matching Products to Needs – Borrowers, Financing Requirements, Facilities and Taxation.

Topic 4

Review questions, activity and case study

The following review questions, activity and case study are designed to increase your understanding of the material you have just studied.

◆ The **review questions** are designed so that you can check your understanding of this topic.

◆ Completion of the **activity** will give you further opportunity to research and understand, in more depth, the themes running through this topic.

◆ The **case study** encourages you to think further about the application of the content of this topic.

The answers to the questions and case study are provided at the end of these learning materials. Please note that the activity is open-ended and therefore a suitable 'answer' may not be provided.

Review questions

1. Examine some of the purposes for which the following types of lending can be extended.

   ◆ Bridging finance.

   ◆ Mortgage finance.

2. Examine the importance of forecasting for working capital requirements.

3. What are the sources of finance for purchasing current and fixed assets?

Activity

Activity 1

> Examine applications for finance from a number of your customers and consider why they needed to borrow (if at all) and where the potential might be for them to borrow in future.

Case study

LA Gear was a company that manufactured fashion footwear. It designed glamorous workout shoes and casual footwear, and used glamorous models to market its products. Its rise was meteoric. In 1988, it was ranked number three on *Business Week*'s list of best small companies. In 1989 it was the top performing company on the New York Stock Exchange (NYSE) and was valued at over $1bn. The company was able to cater successfully to the demands for fashion 'excesses' of the 1980s – but it failed to predict the more austere lifestyle trends of the early 1990s and suffered massive losses.

The company was able to fund operating losses by sale of marketable assets. By managing its working capital and selling excess inventories, it kept going for a number of years. Despite strict loan covenants and large losses, the company was able to survive for a considerable length of time due largely to the liquidity of its asset base. LA Gear's highly liquid asset structure enabled it to meet its debt obligations despite falling revenues.

Although in the case of LA Gear the high degree of asset liquidity did not save it from ultimate collapse in 1998, DeAngelo et al (2002) who researched the company conclude that asset liquidity is beneficial and is able to give a company management time to implement a successful turnaround. A high degree of asset liquidity – particularly the ability to liquidate working capital – might enable a company to survive financial difficulties for a considerable length of time.

1 What was the primary reason for the decline in the sales of LA Gear in the 1990s?

2 Why is it necessary for a lender to have a good knowledge of the industry in which a borrowing company operates?

3 Why was the company able to survive for a number of years despite heavy losses?

4 What is the significance of having asset liquidity in times of financial distress?

Topic 5
Forms of lending

Learning outcomes

By the end of this topic, students should be able to understand the importance of matching products with needs, and the features and benefits of a range of secured and unsecured lending products.

Learning areas include:

◆ overdrafts;

◆ loans;

◆ credit cards;

◆ debtor finance (invoice discounting and factoring);

◆ asset finance (hire purchase and leasing);

◆ other forms of finance, including equity finance and government-backed loan guarantee schemes.

5.1   Types of lending

It is important to match lending products to the needs of individual consumers. Borrowers need to be targeted with the right products. The lender needs to be flexible in a number of areas in order to match borrower requirements, including:

◆ size;

◆ availability;

◆ repayment terms;

◆ delivery methods;

◆ seasonality and time of requirement;

◆ level of security;

◆ form of lending.

Lending can therefore take a range of forms and these forms can vary in nature and complexity. Figure 5.1 illustrates some of the ways in which lending can be classified.

Figure 5.1   Lending classifications

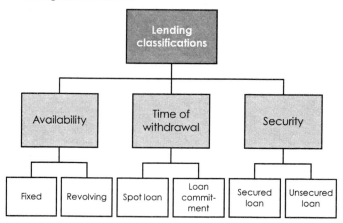

Successful lending requires the successful matching of lending products with consumer needs. The lender therefore needs to be aware of the various forms in which lending can be extended.

These types of lending outlined in section 5.1.1 to section 5.1.5 can be structured to suit the needs of a variety of borrowers ranging from an individual who requires a small personal loan to a large corporate requiring a syndicated loan that involves the participation of many lenders.

5.1.1   Fixed and revolving credit

Fixed credit is granted for a fixed amount and reduces when loan repayments are made, whereas **revolving credit** reverts to its original credit limit when repayments are made. 'Revolving' means turning around, or reverting, to some pre-established point. Revolving credit is a credit line that is available to a borrower on a revolving basis: loan withdrawals and loan repayments can be made as often as required within the stipulated credit limit, and the availability of credit is dependent upon credit repayments.

5.1.2   Spot loan and loan commitments

A **spot loan** is withdrawn immediately in full, whereas a **loan commitment** can be withdrawn as and when required in instalments over a stipulated time period, for example, building progress payments.

5.1.3   Secured and unsecured advances

A **secured advance** is backed by security such as land or shares, whereas an **unsecured advance** is not backed by any specified security. A secured lender has first claim on the specified security in the event of default or insolvency, whereas an unsecured lender has only a general claim on the assets of the borrower in the event of default or insolvency. Because unsecured loans involve a higher degree of risk to the lender, these loans will attract a higher rate of interest charges and fees in order to compensate the lender for the higher amount of risk involved.

5.1.4 Single payment loans and instalment loans

A **single payment loan** is repaid in one lump sum, whereas **instalment credit** is repaid over more than one instalment.

5.1.5 Syndicated loans

A **syndicated loan** is one given by a group of lenders as against a single lender.

5.2 Overdrafts

> An **overdraft** is a credit facility whereby a lender allows a borrower to exceed the amount deposited or to borrow up to, or over, a specified limit, subject to the payment of interest and other charges.

Overdrafts are usually permitted in a current account. The funds in a **current account** are repayable on demand and are therefore also known as **'on demand' accounts**. In some countries, such as the USA and Canada, it is known as a **checking account**, because the funds in the account can be paid out or withdrawn by using cheques. It should be noted that different laws apply in the US, where it is an offence to issue cheques without having credit balances to meet them – thus precluding the use of overdrafts. More recent methods of withdrawing or paying out funds from these accounts include the electronic debit card or via an automated teller machine (ATM). Direct debits and standing orders can be set up in a current account whereby funds can be automatically paid out to designated parties at regular intervals as required.

Overdrafts are granted to a variety of customer types such as individuals, partnerships and corporates. Although an overdraft is regarded as short-term finance, many customers operate a core overdraft on an almost permanent basis. An overdraft generally falls within the Consumer Credit Act 1974, Sch 2, definition of 'a regulated consumer credit agreement for unrestricted use running account credit'.

5.2.1 Features of an overdraft

An overdraft is a credit facility generally granted in a running current account. It can be an agreed overdraft limit according to prior arrangement, or an unauthorised overdraft allowed by the lender when the account holder issues a cheque over and above the amount of credit available in the account. In *Cuthbert v Robarts Lubbock and Co* [1909] it was held that when a customer draws a cheque in excess of the amount available in the account, it is deemed to be a request for credit and, if a bank allows the excess payment, the customer is deemed to have borrowed money from the bank. Unauthorised overdrafts are usually charged higher fees and interest.

An overdraft is a commitment whereby the borrower is able to draw funds as and when required. Thus the borrower can avoid making use of the limit altogether if so desired.

It is a revolving credit whereby any repayments restore the limit available for future withdrawals.

It is generally unsecured, unless the lender has entered into a prior arrangement whereby security is obtained. An unsecured overdraft limit may therefore be charged higher interest and fees than a secured facility.

According to the rule in *Clayton's Case* (*Devaynes v Noble* [1816]), first credits into an account repay first debits out, in chronological order. In *Clayton's Case*, there was a substantial debit balance in a partnership's account when one of the partners died, but the firm continued running as a going concern. Eventually, the bank became insolvent, but Clayton, a surviving partner, was unable to recover money due to him from the deceased partner's estate, because it was held that subsequent credits had gone to towards extinguishing the liability of the deceased partner's estate towards the partnership firm.

An overdraft is generally repayable on demand unless otherwise specified, but the lender's right to immediate repayment cannot unduly prejudice the legitimate rights of the borrower (Arora, 1997). Here are some examples of case law relating to overdrafts. In *Rouse v Bradford Banking Co* [1894] it was held that if a bank has agreed to give an overdraft, it cannot refuse to honour cheques or drafts, within the limit of that overdraft, which have been drawn and put into circulation before any notice to the person to whom it has agreed to give the overdraft that the limit is to be withdrawn. Thus the lender is required to give the borrower reasonable notice to make repayment (*Joachimson v Swiss Bank Corpn* [1921]; *RA Cripps and Son Ltd v Wickenden* [1973]). The debtor is not in default unless and until they have been given an opportunity to arrange for the 'mechanics of payment' that might be needed to repay the debt, but if the lender is not required to extend any further time to the borrower for raising money if the money is not available for making payment (*Bank of Baroda v Panessar* [1987]). Thus where a borrower who has received a demand for the repayment of an overdraft informs the bank that they do not have sufficient funds to repay in full the lender can treat the customer as being in default and can take immediate legal action.

Where a customer has two or more accounts with the same bank the bank has the common law right to set off any credit balance held against any debit balances. (*Garnett v McEwen* [1872]). This applies even if the accounts are held at different branches. The bank is free to choose which overdrawn accounts will be combined; ie if there is a debit balance on a current account and credit balance on another current account these can be combined to ascertain the net balance. If there is more than one debit account the bank can choose which account to set-off against the credit balance. If, for example, it held the previously mentioned accounts and also an overdrawn wages account (s 386 of the Insolvency Act 1986) then, to preserve its preferential claim in the event of insolvency, the bank will not set-off the credit balances against the wages account.

If the customer is subject to insolvency then the provisions of the Insolvency Act 1986, s 323 apply. The bank's right of set-off becomes a statutory right under the provisions of the Act. Under statutory set-off the bank loses the right to choose to which account to apply the credit balance, in the event of there being more than one debit balance the credit balance must be apportioned rateably between the debit accounts.

5.2.2 Features of overdrafts

◆ The lender is able to generate income in the form of interest and fees. As overdrafts are generally unsecured, the lender charges higher interest charges and fees to compensate for the increased level of risk involved. Lenders charge even higher fees and penal rates of interest when limits are overdrawn without prior arrangement.

◆ The rate of interest will usually be linked to an underlying base rate and will vary with that rate. Lenders can vary the margin above the base rate to reflect the risk involved. The lender is also able to reserve the right to change the rate even if the reference rate has not changed, or to effect a change that is higher than the change in the reference rate.

◆ In larger overdraft agreements, the lender is able to levy non-utilisation fees on the amounts of the facility not being used.

◆ Overdrafts are generally renewable annually, and lenders are able to review the borrower's creditworthiness at this time.

◆ Unless there is a prior arrangement whereby the overdraft has been granted for a fixed period, the lender can demand repayment at any time. Overdrafts are generally repayable on demand and the lender retains the right to call up the overdraft subject to giving a reasonable time to the borrower to repay the debt.

◆ The lender is able to generate high volumes of lending in the form of overdrafts, because these are an extremely popular form of borrowing due to the following factors:

  – ease of use and flexibility;

  – ease of access;

  – speed of access;

  – interest is usually payable only on the outstanding balances and not on the entire limit.

◆ There is a higher risk of credit default on any overdrafts that are unsecured.

◆ Interest is generally payable only on the amount drawn by the borrower.

◆ Being a credit commitment, the lender will find it difficult to predict its usage and income flow. Unexpected withdrawals can be a source of increased liquidity risk and can make liquidity management more difficult for the lender.

5.3 Loans

A **loan** is usually made available on a fixed and spot basis and can be secured or unsecured.

A loan falls within the Consumer Credit Act 1974 definition of 'a regulated consumer credit agreement for restricted or unrestricted use fixed sum credit'. This does not apply to loans to limited companies.

5.3.1 Features of loans

Loans are offered for specified amounts for specified periods. The lender cannot seek repayment prior to expiry of the period unless there has been some default, eg in payment of periodic interest. Similarly, the borrower may be unable to repay early without incurring early redemption penalties. In the absence of a specified period the lender will need to give the borrower a notice of repayment giving a reasonable period for paying back the loan (*Buckingham and Co v London and Midland Bank* [1895]). Where a loan is advanced for a specified purpose and the loan agreement does not deal with repayment, the lender cannot withdraw the loan before the purpose is achieved (*Williams and Glyn's Bank Ltd v Barnes* [1980]). It is therefore important that lenders specify a repayment period in such a way that it does not give rise to any ambiguity.

Loans can made available in the short term for periods of a year or less, or for longer terms ranging up to 25 years or more. Short-term loans can be made to fund consumer durables, while long-term loans such as mortgages can fund house purchases and corporate projects.

5.3.2 Advantages of loans

◆ The lender is able to generate income in the form of interest and fees. In addition to interest, the lender is able to charge an initial arrangement or commitment fee and other fees, and also to obtain some protection against unanticipated loan closures in the form of early redemption fees.

◆ Interest is paid on the full amount of the outstanding loan and the lender is not faced with a situation in which an agreed credit facility is unutilised or underutilised, as may be the case with overdrafts.

◆ Where loans are secured against a fixed charge on the asset being financed, the risk is lower and lenders are able to compete for business by charging competitive rates of interest.

◆ Lenders are able to reduce risk even further by requiring the borrower to take out insurance.

◆ The lender is able to arrange for legally binding covenants before agreeing to a loan. For example, the borrower may be required to keep the overall gearing or debt below a certain level. If the conditions are breached, the bank will be entitled to immediate repayment.

◆ The lender is able to lend a fixed sum of money for a definite period, and is therefore able to anticipate earnings and make funding arrangements for a definite period.

◆ The lender is able to generate high volumes of lending in the form of loans, because these are an extremely popular form of borrowing due to the following factors:

  – the term of a loan can be matched to the life of any asset to be purchased;

  – loan repayments can be tailored to match the cash flow of the project;

  – the interest rate on loans can be fixed, allowing borrowers to forecast interest costs with a greater degree of certainty.

5.3.3 Disadvantages of loans

◆ There is always a risk that the borrower might fail to make repayments in accordance with the agreed programme or breach any of the covenants, and that the security available might not cover the recovery costs.

◆ Some loan products are particularly high risk. The following products have been identified by the FSA as higher risk products and areas:

– equity release products, under which the equity in an asset, such as a house, is released to the residents subject to repayment being made from the sale of the property on the death of the owners;

– the sub-prime sector, within which loans are extended to borrowers with poor credit histories;

– interest-only products, for which no provision has been made for the repayment of the principal;

– self-certification products, where not much attempt is made to verify the veracity of the claims made by borrowers in relation to their income and sources of repayment.

These higher risk products are characterised by a combination of product complexity, potential customer vulnerability and lock-ins. Lenders are required to be particularly careful to ensure that the risks and features of products are clearly explained and that customers obtain appropriate advice.

5.4 Credit cards

A **credit card** is an revolving loan commitment that is usually unsecured. It is a plastic card that can be identified by a magnetic strip and/or chip, which is issued by a lending institution authorising the holder to buy goods and services on credit up to a specified limit.

5.4.1 Features of credit cards

A credit card involves 'a debtor–creditor–supplier agreement'. There are at least three parties to credit card lending:

◆ the card issuer;

◆ the card holder;

◆ the supplier who accepts the card in payment for goods and services supplied.

Under a four-party structure, there is also the independent merchant acquirer, who recruits new suppliers willing to accept the issuer's card. Under this arrangement, the merchant acquirer accepts payment for the products or services on behalf of the merchant and undertakes to pay the supplier and the card issuer.

A credit card is issued for a specified credit limit. A period of interest-free credit is specified, beyond which interest will become payable at a specified rate. Subject to prior arrangements, the borrower will have the option of either paying off the entire credit balance within the interest-free credit period, or paying a minimum required amount and interest on the remaining amount at a specified rate. There is usually a sub-limit for cash withdrawals and interest is payable from date of cash withdrawal.

A credit card provides revolving credit, which allows card holders to make purchases and repayments as often as required within the stipulated credit limit.

Lenders' income arises from three sources:

♦ any arrangement fee charged;

♦ the interest on balances outstanding beyond the interest free period;

♦ the fees paid by merchants who supply the goods paid for by credit cards;

There are more than 300 credit cards in the UK and lenders offer a variety of incentives:

♦ balance transfer cards offer special interest rates for a specified balance transfer period or for the life of the balance amount transferred from another card provider. Other variations are an initially low rate for purchases and a combination of purchases and balance transfers;

♦ loyalty reward cards offer rewards, such as airmiles, for card usage;

♦ cashback cards offer cash back set as a fixed percentage of the amount spent;

♦ ethical cards undertake to donate a percentage of the card spend for charity.

5.4.2 Advantages of credit cards

♦ Lenders are able to charge high rates of interest and fees, and these rates do not seem to deter borrowers.

♦ Credit cards facilitate quick and easy payments and their increasing use has been reflected in increased earnings for card issuers.

♦ Credit cards appeal both to borrowers who wish to avoid or minimise interest payments by early settlement and to those who wish to take advantage of the maximum credit periods on offer.

♦ Lenders receive commission from merchant suppliers on every credit card transaction.

♦ There is scope for increased automation and reduced paperwork.

5.4.3 Disadvantages of credit cards

♦ Not all retailers accept credit cards, although the number that do not is decreasing.

♦ While lenders are able to earn high interest when repayments are limited to the small amount specified as the minimum requirement each month, this has led to long-term indebtedness and increased costs for borrowers in the form of compounded interest, resulting in further adverse publicity.

◆ There is also the negative public perception that credit cards involve a hidden expense on all transactions conducted by merchants, who accept credit cards because they must build the cost of transaction fees into their overall business expense, thereby increasing the cost for all purchasers, including cash and other non-credit-card-using customers.

◆ As discussed in section 2.1.2, the issuer of a credit card becomes jointly and severally liable for misrepresented or defective goods sold by a supplier in terms of the principle of 'connected lender liability' established by s 75 of the Consumer Credit Act 1974. (FOS, 2003.)

5.5   Debtor finance

Debtor finance is usually made available on a revolving basis as a line of credit and is secured by an assignment of book debts. Invoices/ bills are assets representing underlying trade transactions. Invoice discounting is consequently a form of secured or asset-based lending (ABL), or debtor finance. It is a form of lending that provides an advance against outstanding invoices or accounts receivable.

Invoice discounters (and factors) take an assignment of their client's book debts, thereby assuming legal title to the debt and its proceeds. Collections are also received into blocked accounts and the *Brumark* ruling (see section 9.5.2) is therefore not likely to affect the security held by invoice discounters and factors.

This type of loan is structured as a revolving line of credit. Subject to an overall credit limit, submission of new invoices for discounting will increase the amount outstanding, which will be reduced by payment of invoices on the due date.

5.5.1   Features of debtor finance

An invoice furnishes the details, such as date, seller, buyer, quantities, prices, freight and credit terms, of a transaction. The invoice represents money receivable by the seller from the buyer at a future date that is dependent upon the credit terms of the transaction. While it might be necessary to offer a period of credit to the buyer in order to secure the buyer's order, this delays the realisation of the proceeds of the sale. The seller might therefore wish to offer the invoice to a lender as security for a loan. Alternatively, the seller might be willing to accept a reduced amount of the invoice from the lender immediately and part with a proportion of the invoice known as **discount** in exchange for immediate receipt of cash.

Discount represents the difference between the face value of the invoice and the reduced, but immediate, amount advanced by the lender. Thus an invoice for £1,000 payable after three months might be discounted by the seller with a lender for £980; this means that the seller will receive an immediate cash amount of £980 and the lender will receive the full amount of £1,000 after three months, the £20 representing the discount, or return, for the lender for the period of three months. In this case, the effective interest rate works out to 8% per annum – that is, the rate of interest is 2% per quarter and 8% for four quarters (or per annum).

Sellers offer invoices at a discount because of their need for cash in order to ensure the continued conduct of the business. Thus debtor financing will have three parties to the transaction:

◆ the seller, who originates the invoice;

◆ the buyer, who has an obligation to pay the invoice at a future date;

◆ the discounter or lender.

A characteristic of this type of finance is that lenders will usually retain a margin, and extend advances from 70% of the debtors' ledger value up to 85% or 90%. Higher levels of finance will be available in cases where additional security is on offer.

Debtor finance takes the form of either invoice discounting or factoring, and is often taken up by companies who find that delays in cash flow have created pressure on a bank overdraft facility. While debtor finance will undoubtedly improve receipts into the bank account, it will only provide a single cash injection from the initial advance. Subsequent months will see the normal trade cycle re-established as receipts from invoices repay initial finance and new invoices create new finance.

Debtor finance has taken on increased popularity will lenders following BASEL II as it requires lower liquidity that overdraft lending.

5.5.2 Invoice discounting

◆ While borrowers are able to raise finance on debts, they continue to be responsible for chasing the debts, and hence charges are usually lower than in forms of financing such as factoring, within which the factor company takes on the task of following up on bill payments.

◆ Invoice discounting can be undertaken by a bank directly rather than through a subsidiary, as might have to be the case in relation to factoring and some other forms of finance.

◆ While there is a risk of non-payment of the invoices on the due date, recourse to the customer is available in the event of non-payment, and the lending is therefore relatively safe and low risk.

◆ Lenders are able to achieve increased volumes of this type of lending, because it is popular among customers for a number of reasons:

 – cash flow is improved due to the immediate availability of cash;

 – charges are comparatively low, because the lending is secured;

 – the borrowers are able to choose the bills that they might wish to discount.

◆ Lenders may not discount invoices for small accounts and may be accused of being overly selective.

5.5.3 Factoring

Factoring is a form of debtor finance or accounts receivable financing, similar to invoice discounting, but with some added features.

In addition to benefiting from the receipt of immediate cash from the factor or lender, the seller also passes on the task of debt collection to the factor company.

The factor or lender takes over title to the debts, retains a fee and passes on the remaining value of the invoice collected to the business.

Factoring can be either:

◆ **with recourse**. This means that the factor has recourse to the seller in case of unpaid invoices and can reclaim their value;

◆ **without recourse**. Here the factor buys the invoice and carries the risk of it remaining unpaid. As one might expect, the cost of this service reflects the higher risk involved.

5.5.3.1 Advantages of factoring

◆ Factoring is popular with many businesses, because it improves cash flow and allows time and attention to be focused on the operations of the business, rather than on debt collection.

◆ The factor or lender is able to earn income in the form of fees from the accounting services offered and from factoring debts due. Non-recourse factoring yields an even higher level of income.

◆ Many businesses are interested in this form of finance, because they benefit from the acceleration of cash flow by obtaining cash from the factor that is equal to the face vale of the invoices less the factors fee.

◆ The factor is able to earn fees from ancillary business, such as providing advice on trading terms in export markets, handling correspondence in the language of the overseas debtor, providing assistance with the resolution of disputes, offering protection against exchange risk, etc.

◆ The factor is able to build up a detailed database of information about the creditworthiness of companies with which its clients have dealings. This will help in the assessment of the creditworthiness of new and existing clients, and will also offer a source of income from its advising clients about the potential creditworthiness of trading partners.

◆ Factoring is considered off-balance-sheet financing, in that it is not a form of debt or a form of equity. This enables a factor to extend this form of finance to a borrower even in circumstances under which it will be inappropriate to extend traditional bank and equity financing. In the case of some new or under capitalised companies, it might be the only form of finance that can be extended.

5.5.3.2 Disadvantages of factoring

◆ Factoring can create an unfavourable image of the lender as an unsympathetic debt collector in contrast with the more favourable image of the seller as a sympathetic trade partner. Factoring can discourage some potential buyers who would prefer to deal with the seller directly rather than via a factor, thus harming the financial standing of the seller.

◆ Factoring may impose constraints on the way in which a seller might like to do business. Factors may want to pre-approve potential buyers, causing delays in the trade transactions.

◆ Factoring is perceived to be inflexible. Sellers might be put off by the fact that they cannot choose which invoices to sell to the factor and will have to pay factoring charges for sound debts, while remaining exposed to debts that are less safe.

◆ Factors might be able to take only customers who sell on credit for fairly large amounts at a time. It might not be viable to take on smaller transactions.

◆ Non-recourse factoring can give rise to the risk of bad debts and losses.

5.6 Asset finance

While invoice discounting and factoring facilitate the financing of accounts receivable, **asset finance** facilitates the acquisition of fixed assets such as capital equipment.

As noted in section 4.2.4, fixed assets have a useful economic life spread over a number of years and it will be appropriate to spread the repayment of loans over the period of the life of the asset for which the lending is undertaken. The most common forms of medium term finance for investment in capital assets are hire purchase and leasing.

The following are examples of business assets that may be suitable for financing using hire purchase or leasing:

◆ plant and machinery;

◆ business cars and other vehicles;

◆ office equipment and tools;

◆ computer hardware and software.

Hire purchase is usually made available on a fixed and spot basis, and is secured by the asset that is required to be purchased with the finance.

The borrower/user chooses the equipment required and the lender buys it on their behalf. The user is able to avoid immediate cash outflow for purchase of the asset, the cost of the asset being paid for in instalments over the period of the hire purchase. Under hire purchase, the contract envisages that ownership will ultimately pass to the user of the asset after all of the payments have been made. Consequently, it is more similar to a straight loan, with the user of the asset gaining the benefit of capital allowances. Capital allowances can be a significant tax incentive for businesses. In the case of consumer finance, after payment of a small fee at the end of the contract.

The difference between hire purchase and a straight loan is that, under hire purchase, the repayment instalments are equated as in a mortgage. Hence, the timings of the interest, as well as principal cash flows would differ from those on a straight loan.

The user of the asset is normally responsible for its maintenance.

5.6.1 Features of hire purchase

◆ The lender is able to generate income in the form of fees.

◆ Interest is paid on the full amount of the initial loan, even though the balance outstanding will decline over the term of the loan. Because of the way in which interest is calculated, the true interest is roughly double that of the quoted rate (Pike and Neale, 2006).

◆ Asset finance, like debtor finance, has taken on increasing popularity with lenders following Basel II, due to reduced liquidity requirements when compared to overdrafts.

◆ As loans are secured against a fixed charge on the asset being financed, the risk is comparatively low. In addition, lenders will require the hirer to put down a deposit. It may be possible for the business to 'trade in' other assets that they own, as a means of raising the deposit.

◆ Lenders are able to reduce risk even further by requiring the borrower to take out insurance to cover the asset.

◆ In most cases, the payments are fixed throughout the hire purchase agreement, and the lender is therefore able to anticipate earnings and make funding arrangements for a definite period.

◆ The lender is able to match the repayments with the expected revenue and profits generated by the use of the asset.

◆ As a finance vehicle for consumer goods purchase, hire purchase has largely been replaced by personal loans, but still remains available, and allows lenders to have a charge over the goods purchased.

5.7 Leasing

> A **lease** is defined as a rental agreement between the owner of an asset (the **lessor**) and the user of the asset (the **lessee**).

Until a few years ago, leasing was 'off-balance-sheet' financing, meaning that gearing ratios and return on investment ratios would appear better than they actually were. But with the introduction of SSAP 21, all financial leases should be capitalised and present value of lease rentals payable must be shown as a liability. It is therefore no longer accurate to say that leasing improves gearing and other ratios. Accounting standards, such as IAS 17, FRS 5 and SSAP 21, require that appropriate disclosure is made and that the substance of the transactions is transparent.

Leasing is based on the realisation that it is the use, rather than the ownership, of assets that brings revenue. The lessee has the right to use the asset during the lease term and also the obligation to make specified payments over the lease term. The lessor or the lender who leases out the asset has the rights to receive payments during the lease term and to the residual value of the asset after the lease term has expired.

5.7.1 Features of leasing

As with hire purchase, the lessee is able to avoid immediate cash outflow for the purchase of the asset, the cost of the asset being paid for in instalments over the period of the lease. The main difference from hire purchase is that, under leasing, the ownership never passes to the user of the asset. Ownership continues to remain with the lessor at all times, and the lessor claims the capital allowances and passes some of the benefit on to the lessee by way of reduced rental charges. The lessee is able to deduct the full cost of lease rentals from taxable income, as a trading expense.

There are a variety of types of leasing arrangement. Two major types are as follows.

An **operating lease** is a short-term agreement for renting an asset: the agreement is cancellable during the contract period, and the asset is returned to the lessor well before the expiry of its life. Such leases are entered into mainly for convenience and to avoid the risk of obsolescence in respect of assets such as computers, which tend to become outdated very quickly. Maintenance of the asset is the responsibility of the lessor.

A **finance lease** is a long-term, non-cancellable agreement for renting an asset, for virtually its full economic life. The asset is usually selected by the lessee and is bought by the lessor for the specific purpose of leasing it out to the lessee only. The lessee is usually responsible for maintaining and insuring the asset. A finance lease is, in fact, nothing but a way of financing the purchase of an asset. The UK Accounting Standard SSAP 21 defines it as a lease that 'transfers substantially all the risks and rewards of ownership to the lessee'.

5.7.2 Advantages of leasing

♦ The lender or lessor is able to generate income in the form of lease rentals and fees.

♦ Because the lender retains ownership of the asset at all times, the risk is comparatively low. In addition, lenders will require the lessee to make one or more payments in advance under a lease. Because the lessor retains legal title to the assets, the credit assessment is usually less rigorous, and finance can be released fairly quickly and with fewer restrictions than other forms of finance, such as loans and debentures.

♦ Lenders are able to reduce risk even further by requiring the borrower to take out insurance to cover the asset.

♦ In most cases, the payments are fixed throughout the lease agreement, and the lender is therefore able to anticipate earnings and make funding arrangements for a definite period.

♦ The lender is able to match the repayments with the expected revenue and profits generated by the use of the asset. There is a lot of flexibility in structuring the lease rentals. Depending on the cash flow needs of the lessee, the lease payments can be 'front ended' (larger payments in the beginning of the lease period) or 'back ended' (the rentals increase over the lease period).

♦ Leasing offers both the lender and the borrower opportunity for tax trading, particularly if the lessee is not in a tax paying position or pays corporation tax at the small companies rate. One of the important incentives for investment in assets is the capital allowance, which is deducted from a firm's taxable income;

if the lessee is tax-exhausted (has no further scope for deducting anything from taxable income), however, capital allowance has to be carried forward, deferring the advantage of the tax deduction and reducing the present value of the benefit. Even if the lessor is not tax-exhausted, differences in tax status can offer scope for tax trading. The lessor can pass on a part of the tax benefit to the lessee through reduced lease rentals.

5.7.3 Disadvantages of leasing

◆ Many borrowers, particularly those who are generating good profits, are concerned that the asset does not become the outright property of lessee and that they will be unable to use the capital allowances as they would in the case of hire purchase or outright purchase.

◆ Disposal of assets at the end of the leasing period may be difficult if the lessee does not want to continue use.

5.8 Other forms of providing finance

5.8.1 Equity finance

Participating in the equity of a company can be an alternative to lending as a way of providing finance.

> **Equity** is the ordinary share capital of a company. **Equity finance** is the provision of finance in the form of equity or ordinary share capital in a company.

Equity finance is share capital invested in a business for the medium to long term in return for a share of the ownership and an element of control of the business. Equity finance is also known as **venture capital**, or **risk capital**, indicating the high risk of providing this form of capital to new business ventures as discussed in section 4.2.1. The provider of such finance will be a part-owner rather than a lender and will have a right to participate in the future profits of the business. Banks, private equity firms and 'business angels' are known to provide equity finance to upcoming business ventures, and often also share in the management and control of the business.

5.8.1.1 Advantages of equity finance

◆ Lenders can widen the range of their product offering by making available funds in the form of equity finance.

◆ There is potential for high returns. Equity finance can be used for high-growth businesses that eventually achieve flotation on the stock market or are sold for a high price, resulting in rich rewards for the equity financiers.

◆ Equity finance provides an alternative source of funding, especially in situation in which other forms, such as bank loans, cannot be made available. In certain circumstances, equity finance might be more appropriate than other forms of finance. A borrower with a high level of debt might not qualify for additional lending. Some businesses may not have enough cash to pay loan interest because available cash needs to be allocated for core activities or for funding growth.

◆ As part-owners, equity financiers have a vested interest in the profitability and growth of the business, because they will be better able to realise their investment through flotation or sale if the business is doing well. In addition to funds, they can bring other valuable resources such as skills, contacts and experience, to the business and can assist with strategy and key decisionmaking. The business can also benefit from the discipline provided by the close scrutiny and evaluation of potential investors.

5.8.1.2 Disadvantages of equity finance

◆ The funding is committed to the business and its projects, and cannot be recalled as can be a loan.

◆ Arranging equity finance is demanding and time-consuming. The business will be required to submit comprehensive information that will need to be scrutinised. Ongoing management time will need to be set aside to study the information for monitoring purposes.

◆ Equity finance is high risk: shareholders rank much lower than creditors in the order of liquidation. The probability of losing the investment is high. It is because equity investors share in the risks of the business that equity finance is often referred to as risk capital.

◆ No interest is receivable as it is in loans. Unlike lenders, equity finance investors do not normally have rights to interest or to be repaid at a particular date. Their return is usually in the form of dividend payments, which depend on the growth and profitability of the business. Dividends need not be paid unless the business is earning profits.

◆ There might be long delays before any return is available on the money invested.

◆ There can be legal and regulatory issues to comply with when arranging finance.

◆ Equity financiers may find small companies to be unviable. The Wilson Committee (1979) pointed out that small businesses find it difficult to raise venture capital. If a firm's management team is largely restricted to family members, it may find it more difficult to attract equity finance because of the potential difficulties faced by external shareholders in monitoring and controlling the activities of the owner-managers.

◆ Many companies are reluctant to obtain equity finance because:

  – they will be subject to varying degrees of influence over the management of their business and the making of major decisions;

  – their share in the business will be diluted by the introduction of additional equity.

5.8.2 Government-backed loan guarantee scheme

Some small and medium enterprises (SMEs) may be unable to obtain conventional loans because they do not have assets to offer as security. The **Small Firms Loan**

Guarantee (SFLG) helps to overcome this by providing lenders with a government guarantee against default in certain circumstances. The scheme has been in operation since 1981; following the recommendations of the Graham Review, a number of changes to the scheme were bought into force in December 2005.

Some of the features of the SFLG are as follows.

◆ The SFLG is a joint venture between the government Department for Business, Enterprise and Regulatory Reform (BERR) and a number of participating lenders. Participating lenders administer the eligibility criteria and make all commercial decisions regarding borrowing.

◆ The SFLG focuses on newer businesses. The Graham Review recognised that start-ups and young businesses face greater difficulty in accessing finance than established businesses, primarily because they often have an unproven business concept, have had least opportunity to build up a financial track record and have fewer assets against which to secure borrowing. The Review recommended that the eligibility for SFLG should be limited to start-ups and early stage businesses. Therefore the guarantee is available to qualifying UK businesses with an annual turnover of up to £5.6m and which are up to five years old. The 'Five Year rule' is the requirement that a business must have been trading for no more than five years.

◆ The SFLG is available for meeting working capital requirements or for funding capital expenditure, especially if the business does not yet have collateral with which to secure a conventional loan.

◆ A government guarantee to the lender covers 75% of the loan amount, for which the borrower pays a 2% premium on the outstanding balance of the loan to BERR.

◆ The guarantee is extended to loans from a minimum amount of £5,000 up to a maximum of £250,000, and with loan terms ranging to a minimum of two years and a maximum of ten years.

◆ Drawdown can take place in stages to suit the cycles of the business.

◆ Loans can be taken out at variable and fixed rates.

◆ The guarantee is available to businesses in most sectors and for most business purposes.

The changes made to the SFLG scheme in 2005 were expected to create a lending system that is fairer to those early stage businesses that require this type of funding the most, as well as to make the application and awarding process more transparent.

Conclusion

Lending can therefore take a range of forms. Fixed credit is granted for a fixed amount and reduces when loan repayments are made, whereas revolving credit reverts to its original credit limit when repayments are made. A spot loan is withdrawn immediately in full, whereas a loan commitment can be withdrawn as and when required in required instalments over a stipulated time period. A single payment loan is repaid in one lump sum, whereas instalment credit is repaid over more than one instalment.

Successful lending requires the successful matching of lending products with consumer needs. The lender therefore needs to be aware of the various forms in which lending can be extended and their relative advantages and disadvantages. Some of these forms include overdrafts, loans, credit cards, invoice discounting, factoring, hire purchase, leasing and equity finance.

Some small and medium enterprises (SMEs) may be unable to obtain conventional loans because they do not have assets to offer as security. The Small Firms Loan Guarantee (SFLG) helps to overcome this by providing lenders with a government guarantee against default in certain circumstances.

While there is continuing debate as to whether or not government intervention in the credit market is warranted, research has shown that loan guarantees seem to make positive contributions; loans that support the expansion of small enterprises may convey significant benefits to the borrowing firms and, through job creation and retention, to the rest of society (Riding and Haines, 2001).

Further reading

Financial Ombudsman Service (2003) 'Credit cards: equal liability under section 75 of the Consumer Credit Act 1974', *Ombudsman News*, 31, 7–10.

Topic 5

Review questions, activities and case study

The following review questions, activities and case study are designed to increase your understanding of the material you have just studied.

◆ The **review questions** are designed so that you can check your understanding of this topic.

◆ Completion of the **activities** will give you further opportunity to research and understand, in more depth, the themes running through this topic.

◆ The **case study** encourages you to think further about the application of the content of this topic.

The answers to the questions and case study are provided at the end of these learning materials. Please note that the activities are open-ended and therefore suitable 'answers' may not be provided.

Review questions

1. How are overdrafts different from loans? Examine the distinguishing features.

2. Examine the benefits of invoice discounting and factoring as forms of debtor finance.

3. Distinguish between 'debt finance' and 'equity finance'. When would equity finance be appropriate?

4. Examine the main features of the Small Firms Loan Guarantee (SLG) scheme administered by the department for Business, Enterprise and Regulatory Reform (BERR).

Activities

Activity 1

> Visit the website of the Financial Ombudsman Service and read some of the complaints received and settled by them in relation to credit cards under the principle of connected lender liability at http://www.financial-ombudsman.org.uk/publications/ombudsman-news/31/creditcards-31.htm.

Activity 2

> Study a selection of brochures or Internet sources detailing the products offered by your own organisation.

Case study

> Lending has become global. Major card issuers, such as Visa and MasterCard, have developed complex networks that span the globe. Borrowers are able to use these cards in a number of countries over the world. Moreover the Internet has become a popular place to buy goods and it is difficult to determine the place of transactions when payments are effected on the Internet.
>
> Section 75 of the Consumer Credit Act 1974 established the principle of 'connected lender liability' whereby credit card issuers are liable for payments for products and services worth between £100 and £30,000, individually and jointly with suppliers, if a consumer has a valid claim against the supplier for misrepresentation or breach of contract relating to goods or services bought with a credit card. The consumer can make a claim against the credit card issuer as well as, or instead of, the supplier. In view of the increasing globalisation of lending in general, and of credit card use in particular, the question arose as to whether credit card payments made abroad would be covered by the principle of connected lender liability.
>
> The Office of Fair Trading, Lloyds Bank plc and some other banks desired to clarify the grey area and to test in courts the applicability of connected lender liability to card payments made abroad. In November 2004, the High Court held that it did not apply. In March 2006, the Court of Appeal reversed the earlier decision and held that it did. Saxby (2006), who researched the case, concludes that without doubt consumers 'will continue adding by credit card to the £12.5 billion spent in 2004 on overseas transactions'. In October 2007, the

House of Lords upheld the Court of Appeal's decision. The case has clarified that the lender is liable for any misrepresentation of breach of contract on the part of suppliers abroad when the payment of goods and services have been made by cards issued in the UK.

Accordingly, a lender who has provided a credit card to a UK borrower will be liable if, for example, such a borrower uses the card abroad to pay for the hire of a defective car that results in accidental damage to property and even to life.

The complaint below, reproduced from the Financial Ombudsman Service (FOS) website, recounts the case of Mr J who had bought a gold watch while he had been abroad on holiday in Turkey. He said that he had been told it was an expensive designer brand when he paid £1,000 for it, using his credit card, but, shortly after he returned home, the watch stopped working. Mr J eventually got the watch repaired at a cost of £65, at which time, the repairer told him that it was a fake and worth very much less than he had paid for it. Mr J then asked his bank to refund the difference between the amount he paid for the watch and the amount the repairer said it was worth. When the bank refused to meet his claim, Mr J approached the FOS. He said that the watch had been misrepresented as a designer make and that, under s 75 of the Consumer Credit Act, he was entitled to a refund from his credit card company. The FOS found that there was no evidence to support Mr J's allegation of misrepresentation on the part of the retailer in Turkey. None of the documents that he was given when he bought the watch described it as a designer make. The UK repairer confirmed that the watch was made of 18ct gold and it was specified as such in the sales documents. So there did not appear to have been any breach of contract. Even if the transaction had happened in the UK, s 75 would not have applied.

1   What is 'connected lender liability'?

2   What will be considered to be a valid claim for connected lender liability to apply?

3   Was Mr J's claim recounted by the FOS valid? Give reasons.

4 What is the implication to a lender of the ruling made by the House of Lords in October 2007 in relation to the case filed by the Office of Fair Trading on connected lender liability?

Topic 6

The lending cycle – the credit granting process

Learning outcomes

By the end of this topic, students should be able to understand the life cycle of a lending facility, the analysis of a lending proposal and the credit granting process.

For ease of reference, the word 'loan' in this topic should be read to apply to any request for borrowing facilities.

Learning areas include:

◆ the lending cycle;

◆ loan application;

◆ loan evaluation;

◆ loan documentation;

◆ further advances.

6.1 The lending cycle

Lending comprises a succession of or a recurring series of events.

In its brief form, the lending cycle consists of:

◆ the credit granting process;

◆ the credit monitoring process;

◆ the credit recovery process.

Figure 6.1 The brief lending cycle

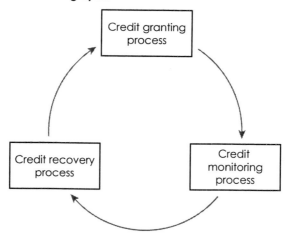

The first of these stages – the credit granting process – is discussed in this topic while the second and third stages are covered in Topic 9.

6.1.1 The credit granting process and principles

The **credit granting process** is the first stage in the lending cycle, and it consists, in turn, of a series of stages:

- ◆ **lead generation**, at which stage the lender attempts to attract the interest of potential borrowers;

- ◆ the submission of a **loan application** by entities wishing to borrow;

- ◆ **loan evaluation** of these applications by lenders;

- ◆ **loan approval** (or rejection).

These stages comprise the credit granting process, or loan origination process, whereby loans are granted to interested applicants considered by lenders to be creditworthy.

Figure 6.2 The credit granting process

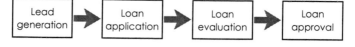

As seen in section 1.5, key principles relating to the credit granting process are:

- ◆ operating within sound, well-defined credit-granting criteria;

- ◆ a thorough understanding of the loan proposal in relation to the:

- − borrower,
- − purpose,
- − structure of the credit,
- − source of repayment;
- ◆ establishing overall credit limits for:
  - − individual borrowers,
  - − groups of connected borrowers,
  - − types of exposures, eg for a particular industry;
- ◆ establishing guidelines for:
  - − approving new credit limits,
  - − renewing or amending existing credit limits,
  - − mitigating risk and ensuring fairness.

6.1.2 Primary security – the borrower

For the lender, the **primary security** for a loan is the borrower's personal covenant to repay. Lenders primarily depend on the borrower's integrity and intentionality and ability to repay the loan. A loan given purely against the primary security of the borrower is an **unsecured loan**, while a loan that is additionally secured by security, such as shares or property, is a **secured loan. Security** is considered to be an insulation against default. Any tendency among borrowers to default wilfully is discouraged by the presence of adequate security – but it will not be good lending practice to grant a loan based purely on the strength of security without taking into account the borrower's integrity and intention to repay the amounts borrowed.

6.2 The loan application and supporting information

6.2.1 The loan application

Other than for some forms of lending such as overdrafts, where lenders are able to offer credit facilities without any formal application, the prospective borrower is required to submit an application for credit facilities on a prescribed form. **Application forms** are carefully drawn up with the assistance of solicitors in order to comply with legal and regulatory requirements. While many application forms are standardised, the format of the application forms will differ depending upon the nature of the credit facility sought. Applicants are required to collect the relevant form from a branch office or download it from the Internet and submit the completed form to the lender, along with supporting documentation to prove their identity and financial status.

6.2.2 Supporting information

In order to originate good quality loans, lenders need to collect relevant and timely information about the prospective borrower and the activity for which the loan is sought. Information can be either 'hard' or 'soft'.

◆ **Hard information** is that which is available from financial statements and other published sources (for example, audited accounts).

◆ **Soft information** is that which is gained about a borrower through ongoing relationships. Such information will be particularly important in lending to small and new private firms because these firms lack a long track record and may not report financial information in a consistent manner. Soft information is used in conjunction with financial and other hard data when making credit decisions' (Gonzalez and James, 2007).

Lenders themselves, as well as brokers and middlemen, will have incentives to overstate both the value of assets being financed as well as the borrower's ability to repay. Lenders need to gear reward systems towards loan safety and not just loan size. If a loan officer is rewarded only on the size of the loan granted, the temptation to inflate the loan may be strong. Skewed incentives will tend to generate skewed behaviour. Reckless and lax lending behaviour can be often attributed to skewed incentives.

Lenders need to be wary about incorrect information and fraudulent loan applications. The following are some of the fraudulent practices that have been detected or suspected by lenders (FSA, 2006a).

◆ Fraudulent documentation in relation to bank statements, utility bills, wage slips, passports, driving licenses, etc.

◆ False employment or income details.

◆ Inconsistent information relating to the same applicant, ie various applications made with different incomes/details either to the same lender or lenders within a group.

◆ Links between different loan applicants, eg shared bank accounts and shared addresses.

Lenders need to seek further information and verification of details furnished in application forms in order to deter fraud and to ensure that the information provided is accurate.

Sources of information available to lenders include:

◆ customer interviews/other interaction;

◆ internal sources, held within the lender's own databases;

◆ external sources of Information, available from published records and statements.

Lenders need to use information gathered from all of these sources to assess borrower creditworthiness and borrowing requirements.

The most important information required by lenders when presented with a request for finance is the business plan and the information that directly supports the request.

This will include:

◆ the business history and reputation;

◆ market analysis and target markets;

◆ the financial results and any growth that have proven the viability of the business idea, including:

  − financial statements for the past three years,

  − current financial indicators,

  − personal financial statements of the promoters/partners/principals, in order to demonstrate net worth outside of business,

  − statements pf debts and accounts receivable;

◆ the operating plan, including:

  − current operating facilities and equipment,

  − plans for expansion, eg any new space, new production facilities and new infrastructure, new information technology;

◆ the marketing plan and sales forecast;

◆ the CVs of members of the management team and key personnel, and any additional staffing requirements;

◆ the details of the finance requested, including:

  ◆ amount,

  ◆ purpose,

  ◆ period,

  ◆ details of security offered.

This list is not exhaustive and lenders will specify their own particular requirements. Banks and other lenders issue explanatory booklets and software to enable prospective borrowers to complete the business plan and to provide:

◆ cash flow forecasts;

◆ forecasts of long-term earnings potential;

◆ sensitivity analyses that test the effects of unfavourable developments in sales volumes, profit margins, etc.

Lenders will need to carry out various types of credit analysis in these and other areas.

6.2.3 The interpretation of financial statements

After gathering information, a lender needs to be able to interpret the information. Numbers such as sales, profits and total assets need to be understood in perspective. A lender needs to evaluate the performance of the borrowing business, comparing it with its own past performance as well as with its industry competitors.

Financial statements enable the lender to investigate the position, performance and prospects of a borrower (Pike and Neale, 2006).

♦ The position of the business at a point in time is examined by looking at the **balance sheet**, which is a financial statement of the assets of the business and how these assets have been financed, ie by owned capital and by liabilities owed to others.

♦ The performance of the business over a period of time is examined by looking at the **profit and loss account** which is a financial statement of the income and expenditure and the resulting profit or loss.

♦ The prospects of the business are examined by looking at the **cash flow statement**, which is a financial statement of cash inflows and outflows, and the change in the cash position over a period of time, as well as at the **cash flow forecast**, which shows expected cash receipts and payments for the following year.

Figure 6.3   A simplified balance sheet format

Balance Sheet as on [DATE]	
Current Assets	Current Liabilities
Fixed Assets	Long-term Debt
Intangible Assets	Shareholders Funds
Total Assets = Total Liabilities	

The balance sheet equation can be represented thus.

Balance Sheet Equation	
Current Assets – Current Liabilities = Net Current Assets (Net Working Capital)	Long-term Debt
Fixed Assets + Intangible Assets	Shareholders Funds
Net Assets = Capital Employed	

Comparative ratio analysis, based on financial statements, will help the lender to identify and quantify the borrower's strengths and weaknesses, and to understand the risks to which the borrower might be exposed. A prior knowledge of accounting ratios and methods of calculations is assumed, and a detailed analysis of financial statements is outside the scope of this text. For purposes of ready reference, however, some of the main ratios used for interpreting financial statements are summarised as follows.

Profitability ratios assist the lender in assessing the performance and profitability of the borrower, the adequacy of profits earned and whether profits are increasing or decreasing.

$$\text{Gross profit margin} = \frac{\text{gross profit}}{\text{sales}}$$

$$\text{Net profit margin} = \frac{\text{profit before interest and tax (PBIT)}}{\text{sales}}$$

$$\text{Return on capital employed (ROCE)} = \frac{\text{profit before interest and tax (PBIT)}}{\text{long-term capital}}$$

Activity or asset turnover ratios assist the lender in assessing the efficiency of the use of the assets in terms of sales achieved through the use of these assets.

$$\text{Fixed asset turnover} = \frac{\text{sales}}{\text{fixed assets}}$$

$$\text{Asset turnover} = \frac{\text{sales}}{\text{total assets} - \text{current liabilities}}$$

$$\text{Stockholding period} = \frac{\text{stock}}{\text{cost of sales} \times 365}$$

$$\text{Rate of payment of suppliers (in days)} = \frac{\text{trade creditors}}{\text{cost of sales} \times 365}$$

$$\text{Rate of collection of debtors (in days)} = \frac{\text{debtors}}{\text{credit sales} \times 365}$$

The lender needs to note the period of credit allowed to debtors: too little credit makes it difficult to achieve a satisfactory level of sales, while too much credit reduces the liquidity of the business (Marriott et al, 2002) and makes it more dependent on lenders.

Liquidity ratios, as we have seen in Topic 4, demonstrate the ability of a business to meet its debts as they fall due. Given the importance of the liquidity, how shall we measure it?

Working capital ratio (Current ratio):

$$\text{Working capital ratio (current ratio)} = \frac{\text{Current assets}}{\text{Current liabilities}}$$

$$\text{Acid test ratio (quick ratio)} = \frac{\text{Current assets} - \text{stock}}{\text{Current liabilities}}$$

Both of these ratios are attempting to ascertain the ease with which the business can utilise its current assets to meet the current liabilities. Remember that the current assets are generally cash, stock and debtors and current liabilities are those debts due for payment in less than twelve months. These include trade creditors, overdrafts, and payments received on account. Neither of these definitions is complete.

These ratios are commonly used and there is a consensus opinion that the working capital ratio should be in the region of 2:1 (current assets twice current liabilities) and the acid test ratio should not be less than 1:1 (current assets less stock equals current liabilities). The rationale behind the acid test ratio is that stock can be less liquid than cash or debtors, and as such should be ignored. The usual caveats apply and a current ratio that is acceptable for one type of business will be unacceptable in another. Consider, for example, a supermarket. Its acid test ratio will reflect the fact that it has few, if any, debtors but will have a substantial amount of its current assets in the form of stock. Alternatively, a central heating firm might have a substantial debtor book, but very limited stock.

Investor ratios assess the return available to investors in the business:

$$\text{Earnings per share (EPS)} = \frac{\text{earnings}}{\text{number of equity shares}}$$

$$\text{Price earnings ratio (PE)} = \frac{\text{current share price}}{\text{earnings per share (EPS)}}$$

$$\text{Dividend cover} = \frac{\text{earnings per share (EPS)}}{\text{dividends per share}}$$

$$\text{Return on equity} = \frac{\text{profit before interest and tax (PBIT)}}{\text{shareholders' funds}}$$

Gearing ratios calculate the proportionate contributions of owners and creditors to a business. The **debt equity ratio** indicates the level of outside debt in relation to shareholder funds while:

$$\text{Debt equity ratio} = \frac{\text{debt}}{\text{equity}}$$

OR

$$\text{Debt equity ratio} = \frac{\text{debt}}{\text{debt} + \text{equity}}$$

$$\text{Interest cover} = \frac{\text{profit before interest and tax (PBIT)}}{\text{interest payable}}$$

Interest cover assesses the borrower's ability to meet interest commitments.

Debt has priority in relation to repayment, because creditors need to be repaid before the owners. Also, debt holders need to paid interest before the owners can be rewarded with any dividends. Debt is therefore less risky and hence debt holders will be satisfied with a lower rate of return than will shareholders. Debt also introduces an element of tax savings, because tax is payable only on profits after interest unlike dividends, which are paid out on after-tax profits.

Shareholders are the ultimate risk bearers and have voting rights that give them a say in how a business is run.

For the investor or lender, debt yields interest and shares dividends on both of which income tax is payable; shares might also appreciate in value, which is subject to capital gains tax.

When a business has a high proportion of debt in its capital, it is described as being **highly geared** or **highly leveraged**. Gearing increases the impact of a rise or fall in profits. A rising profits scenario will result in rising returns to shareholders, because interest payable on debt is fixed and the excess profits go to reward the shareholders. Conversely, in a falling profits scenario, shareholders will face increased risk of loss.

The debt equity ratio (see above) indicates the level of outside debt in relation to ordinary share capital.

Generally, lenders will be more willing to extend finance when the level of debt in relation to equity decreases. Gearing ratios assist the lender in assessing risk. The prudent lender will want to examine total borrowing in relation to the equity base and, for this reason, the lender often finds it useful to extend the definition of debt to include loans from directors and bank overdrafts – that is, any debt for which interest is payable. Preference shares are classified by lenders as debt rather than shares as these usually carry fixed rates of interest and have priority on repayment.

6.2.4 Business risk and financial risk

Business risk is the variability of operating profit – that is, **profit before interest and tax (PBIT)**, which, in turn, depends upon a number of factors, such as the:

♦ variability of demand for the products;

♦ variability of selling price;

♦ variability of input costs;

♦ percentage of fixed costs in the cost structure;

♦ ratios facilitate questions rather than provide answers.

Operating gearing is the mix of the variable costs and fixed costs. A business with a larger percentage of fixed costs is said to have a higher degree of operating gearing and this provides a measure of business risk of the borrower.

Financial risk is the variability of net profit available for distribution to shareholders – that is, the additional risk borne by the equity holders as a result of using debt in the capital structure.

Financial gearing is a company's mix of equity and fixed return capital. A business with a large percentage of debt is said to have a high degree of financial gearing, and this provides a measure of its financial risk: the higher the borrowing, the higher the interest payments that must be paid before any remaining earnings can be paid out to equity shareholders as dividends. Financial risk enhances the level of risk over and above the inherent business risk.

There is a trade-off between operating and financial gearing. If there is a high degree of operating gearing, then, unless sales are very stable, it is better to avoid financial gearing, and vice versa. Thus a lender will not like to see a business that has high levels of both business and financial risk.

Lenders use financial ratios in order to look at past performances, as well as to make predictions for the future based on past trends. It is important to note the following while using ratios for analysing company performance.

♦ Ratios can be expressed in a number of different ways, eg as a ratio, as a fraction, as a percentage, etc.

♦ Ratios can be calculated in a number of different ways.

- It is important to be consistent in the method of calculating ratios – otherwise, the results will not be meaningful.

- By themselves, ratios may not convey much meaning; comparisons will need to be made with those of previous years or similar companies in the same industry in order to obtain more meaningful data.

6.2.5 The limitations of financial statements

Lenders need to recognise that financial statements and accounting ratios, while providing useful information about a business, are subject to a number of limitations.

- The figures in financial statements are likely to be at least several months **out of date**, and so will not provide a true picture of the current financial position.

- Financial statements are **summarised versions** of accounting records. The process of summarising may have led to loss of important information that might have been relevant to the user of the information.

- **Inflation** renders comparisons of results over time misleading. What appears to be an improvement in performance might actually be the opposite when figures are adjusted for inflation.

- Financial statements are based on year-end results, which may not always reflect the position during the course of the year. Seasonal businesses often coose the best time of the year to produce financial statements so as to show seemingly better results.

- Financial statements can be **distorted by large, one-off transactions**. It is important to ask for, and to analyse, additional information that might throw light on the implications.

- Too much importance should not be attached to **individual ratios**: some ratios might indicate good performance, while others may signal the opposite. It is important to study a range of financials and to take a balanced view that takes into account any conflicting messages conveyed by financial statements.

- On their own, ratios **are not definitive** and cannot provide an indication of whether they are 'good' or 'bad'. For example, a high current ratio might be 'good', in that it indicates high liquidity, but 'bad' in that it might indicate overstocking, leading to decreased profitability.

- It may be **inappropriate to arrive at thumb-rule conclusions** about the desirability of certain ratios – for example, a current ratio of 2:1 or a debt equity ratio of 2:1 – as what is desirable and the norm in one industry may be entirely different for another industry. For example, supermarkets with a high turnover of stocks might be able to manage with a much lower current ratio than can an engineering firm.

- Meaningful inter-firm comparisons may not be possible even within the same industry, because **every business is unique**, with its own unique set of strengths and weaknesses.

- Even after accounting for intangible assets, **not all of a firm's gains or losses are captured by financial statements**. For example, the arrival or departure of a key staff member may have a significant impact on the profitability of a business, but no impact on the financial statements.

- The choice of **different accounting policies** may distort inter year as well as inter firm comparisons. For example, IAS 16 allows assets to be depreciated at historical cost or revalued. A business may prefer to continue depreciation at historical cost, because revaluation might increase the depreciation charge and result in decreased profits. Different depreciation methods and estimates will report different net income figures in the income statement and different value of assets in the balance sheet. Further, changes in accounting policy may vitiate any comparison of results between different accounting periods.

- **Creative accounting** involves the manipulation of financial numbers usually within the legal framework, but can be used to misrepresent the true financial state of a business.

- **Window dressing** is similar to creative accounting, but sometimes includes illegal activities which are undertaken to camouflage the true state of affairs. Financial ratios can be manipulated or window dressed, and must therefore to be treated with caution.

Financial statements and ratio analysis are useful, but lenders need to be aware of these limitations and make adjustments as necessary. When used with skill and care, however, it is possible to gain from these statements useful insights into the position, performance and prospects of a borrowing business.

6.3   Loan evaluation: tools and techniques

Credit evaluation is important for ensuring loan quality: the accumulation of bad debts can lead to insolvency. Accordingly, lenders use a variety of tools and techniques to evaluate a loan proposal.

6.3.1 CAMPARI and ICE

Lenders use **loan evaluation frameworks** or **checklists** to evaluate a credit application. These **canons of lending**, or **loan criteria**, are expressed in the form of **mnemonics** for easy recall. Mnemonics such as Campari, CCCParts and Parser are used by a number of lending banks.

CAMPARI

C **Character**: integrity, history and background (primary security).

A **Ability**: managerial and technical competence, business ability and legal ability to borrow.

M **Margin (or Means)**: varyingly interpreted as the percentage of loan to value (LTV) of the asset (or profit potential/resources generated by the business). The lower the LTV, the higher the margin available to the lender. The higher the borrower's stake in the business, the lower the risk faced by the lender.

P **Purpose**: purpose for which the finance is required.

A **Amount**: adequacy of amount of loan required and how it will be drawn down.

R **Repayment**: sources from which and period over which loan will be repaid.

I **Insurance**: collateral security offered.

ICE

I   Insurance: both by way of security and life cover.

C   Commission: any fees to be paid.

E   Extras: opportunities for cross-selling other products.

CCCPARTS

C   Character: integrity, history and background (primary security).

C   Capital: the borrower's stake in the business.

C   Capability: managerial and technical competence and business viability.

P   Purpose: purpose for which the finance is required.

A   Amount: adequacy of amount of loan required and how it will be drawn down.

R   Repayment: sources from which and period over which loan will be repaid.

T   Terms: terms and conditions and loan covenants.

S   Security: collateral security offered.

PARSER

P   Person: integrity, history and background (primary security).

A   Amount: adequacy of amount of loan required and how it will be drawn down.

R   Repayment: sources from which and period over which loan will be repaid.

S   Security: collateral security offered.

E   Expertise: managerial and technical competence and business viability.

R   Repayment (or remuneration): sources from which and period over which loan will be repaid (or profit potential generated by the business).

The checklists indicate that lending decisions are largely made on two types of information: knowledge of the past and forecast for the future.

The checklists in section 6.3.1.1 and section 6.3.1.2 are built into credit scoring and other systems devised for determining loan quality and probability of its repayment.

6.3.1.1   Knowledge of the past

◆ Person(s).

  – The background.

  – Managerial skills.

  – Technical skills.

◆ Past financial record.

  – Capital structure or gearing.

  – Working capital or liquidity.

  – Fixed asset or investment.

  – Profitability.

  – Solvency.

6.3.1.2 Forecast for the future

◆ The proposal and its risk.

    – The amount or limit of loan.

    – The purpose for which it is sought.

    – The period for which it is required.

    – The collateral security available.

◆ The projections and probability of repayment.

    – The repayment programme.

    – Interest and other charges.

    – Projected sales and profit.

    – Cash forecasts and budgets.

6.3.2 SWOT and PEST analysis

SWOT is an acronym for Strengths, Weaknesses, Opportunities and Threats. It provides a framework for analysing a business or business idea, and is useful for both lenders and borrowers in reviewing the position and direction of a business proposition.

Strengths and weaknesses relate to the internal structure and working of the business; opportunities and threats relate to the external factors that impact the business.

SWOT analysis is used by lenders to assess a borrower including:

◆ a borrower's position in the market;

◆ the viability of a business proposal;

◆ business planning and strategy;

◆ product, price, distribution method or promotion method;

◆ acquisitions, mergers and partnerships;

◆ a variety of business ideas and strategies.

SWOT analysis is usually presented as a grid comprising four sections under which relevant issues and questions are examined (see Figure 6.4).

SWOT analysis can be accompanied by PESTEL analysis, which examines external factors that might have an impact on the marketing environment of a business.

PESTEL is an acronym for the Political, Economic, Social and Technological and Legal factors that determine the market for a business.

Figure 6.4 The SWOT grid

Strengths	Weaknesses
Unique selling proposition Resources	Reputation Liquidity
Opportunities Niche market Research and development	**Threats** Politcal climate Economic uncertainty

6.3.3 Porter's Five Forces analysis

Lenders will also find Porter's **Five Forces** model useful for analysing the competitive position of a business venture. The model can be used by lenders to assess how:

♦ the threat of new entrants;

♦ the bargaining power of buyers;

♦ the bargaining power of suppliers;

♦ the threat of substitute products; and

♦ rivalry among existing businesses,

affect the competitive position of businesses.

6.3.4 Credit scoring

Credit scoring models are developed by analysing statistics and picking out characteristics that are believed to relate to creditworthiness.

> A **credit score** is expressed as a number that is based on a statistical analysis of a person's current and past credit history, and is used by lenders to evaluate the creditworthiness of that person and the likelihood that the person will meet debt obligations.

Lenders use credit scores to determine who is eligible for a loan, what credit limit should be set and what interest rate should be charged. While credit reporting agencies such as Experian and Equifax adopt different credit scoring models, these are mostly based on scores developed by the Fair Isaac Credit Organization (FICO) to rate credit risk.

The credit score is determined by a complex formula that takes into account about a hundred or more factors. These factors are broadly accounted for by FICO as follows.

◆ 35% – payment history in relation to various accounts such as credit cards and mortgage loans. Credit events such as county court judgments (CCJs), lawsuits, and insolvencies will have an adverse impact on the score.

◆ 30% – the amount of current indebtedness. Having too many credit cards, for example, will have an adverse impact on the score.

◆ 10% – new credit. The number of new credit accounts and the number credit checks that are run on the account will have an adverse impact on the score, on the assumption that a borrower searching for more credit is a greater credit risk.

◆ 15% – the length of the credit history.

◆ 10% – the type of credit.

Figure 6.5 Porter's Five Forces Model

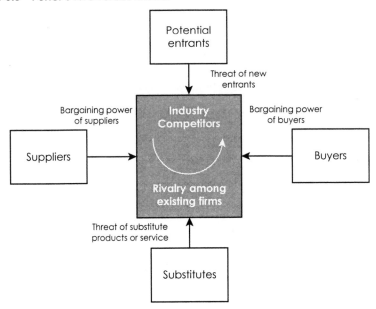

Source: Porter (1980)

A credit score assigned to an individual by a credit scoring organisation generally ranges between 300 and 850: the higher the score, the less risky the borrower; conversely, the lower the score the more risky the borrower. Generally, borrowers are classified as 'prime', 'below prime' or 'poor and unacceptable' based on their sources, as follows:

◆ above 680 – prime loans at competitive rates of interest;

◆ 680–575 – sub-prime loans at higher rates of interest;

◆ below 540 – credit is refused.

Variables, such as occupation, length of employment, length of residence, home ownership status and credit events, will have an impact on the credit score. For example, bankruptcy may result in the deduction of 200 or more points from the credit score.

6.3.4.1 Advantages of credit scoring

◆ Credit scoring provides a consistent mathematical system with which to evaluate prospective and present borrowers.

◆ The credit decision is simplified and the credit-granting process is expedited. Lenders are able to extend credit quickly and at competitive rates to borrowers with higher scores, while rejecting applicants with low scores. More time is available for considering borderline cases.

◆ Lenders are able to adopt a risk-based pricing system, charging interest rates that reflect the level of risk and probability of repayment.

◆ A machine generated score, based on statistical analysis, is likely to be free from bias and, for this reason, applicants are more willing to accept lending decisions based on credit scores.

◆ Rules and criteria can be changed to reflect the current financial climate.

6.3.4.2 Disadvantages of credit scoring

◆ Mathematical, credit scoring systems can still be discriminatory, because they are based on the programmer's subjective judgment, which determines the factors that should be considered and what weight should be assigned to each.

◆ Lenders are not provided with much opportunity for using their credit appraisal skills and lending discretion.

◆ People who have taken breaks in employment (for example, to bring up children), part-time employees and the self-employed may find it difficult to obtain a good score.

◆ Simply shopping around, eg for a better credit card, can have an adverse impact on the score, because multiple enquiries can be construed as potential multiple borrowing.

◆ Credit reports can contain inaccuracies. Individuals with similar names or similar addresses can be lumped together erroneously. Individuals are entitled to complain and set right the position, but this can be a long drawn-out process. It has also been reported that some agencies do not release good information about their sub prime borrowers who repay promptly, so that they are not lured away by competitors.

◆ There are flaws in the concept of credit scoring: for example, a thrifty individual with a complete absence of credit history might find it more difficult to obtain credit than an individual who is more prone to borrowing and spending.

◆ Scoring systems do not incorporate factors, such as general economic conditions, which might create difficulties for debt repayment across a range of borrower categories.

◆ Credit scoring is not fully transparent, despite the right of individuals to ascertain their score for the payment of a small fee.

6.4 Loan documentation and covenants

6.4.1 Loan documentation

Loan documentation is a very important part of the loan approval element in the lending process: an incorrectly or inadequately documented loan may not be enforceable. Lenders need to be able to obtain the relevant documents in a timely and appropriate manner.

The documents need to be:

◆ accurately drawn up, in consultation with qualified solicitors and in strict compliance with legal requirements;

◆ appropriate to the lending activity and loan customer (different activities and customers will require different clauses);

◆ executed by authorised signatories;

◆ obtained in a timely manner (delay in obtaining certain documentation may invalidate the lender's claim);

◆ appropriately recorded and retained in safe custody for reference in case of need.

Some of the more frequently used documents are:

◆ the borrower's application for the grant or renewal of credit facilities;

◆ the corporate borrowing resolution or partnership agreement;

◆ the subordination agreement;

◆ the borrower's and guarantor's financial information and statements;

◆ credit reports;

◆ the loan agreement, signed by the borrower and lender;

◆ evidence of the perfection of security interest;

◆ existing and paid off promissory notes;

◆ insurance policies;

◆ a facility letter advising of the grant of credit;

◆ loan review or renewal documents;

◆ correspondence.

6.4.2 Loan covenants

> A **loan covenant** is a condition with which the borrower must comply in order to adhere to the terms in the loan agreement.

If the borrower does not act in accordance with the covenant, the loan can be considered to be in default and the lender has the right to demand repayment.

Lenders attach covenants to loans as a way of ensuring that borrowers operate in a financially prudent manner and repay the debt. Borrowers, however, would like to negotiate flexible covenants that give them the freedom to make decisions and take risks that might benefit the owners. Setting out loan covenants in a clear manner will benefit both lenders and borrowers, and will ensure that both parties are aware of their duties and obligations.

There are two types of covenant in most loan agreements.

1. **Affirmative covenants** require the borrower to perform certain activities in accordance with the loan terms. Some examples are:

   - repayment of the principal and interest at stipulated intervals;

   - compliance with legal, regulatory and accounting requirements;

   - regular submission of financial statements;

   - prompt payment of taxes, licences and fees;

   - arranging for up to date insurance.

2. **Negative covenants** impose restraints on certain borrower activities. Some examples are limitations on the borrower's freedom to:

   - incur more debt;

   - increase salaries and bonuses;

   - pay large dividends;

   - purchase new assets;

   - effect changes in management.

Covenants can also be operational or financial.

◆ **Operational covenants** can require borrowers to:

   - maintain their physical assets to certain minimum standards;

   - meet minimum disclosure requirements;

- engage only in permissible business activities;

- maintain a minimum level of insurance.

◆ **Financial covenants** can stipulate ratios above or below which the borrower is required to stay. The method of calculating such ratios could be more stringent than those stipulated by accounting standards, for example:

- minimum equity, minimum working capital and maximum debt to equity (leverage);

- minimum quick and current ratios (liquidity);

- minimum Return on Assets and Return on Equity (profitability).

Loan covenants attempt to achieve a variety of objectives such as:

◆ cash flow control;

◆ balance sheet control;

◆ trigger recall or restructuring of the loan. (Hempel and Simonson, 1999.)

Rise in competition and the resultant increase in power of borrowers has led to what is called covenant-lite loans, which are 'light' on the covenants that were otherwise used to safeguard against borrower default. Lenders need to ensure that the 'herd instinct' to follow other lenders is resisted, and the need to stipulate rigorous covenants recognised at all times.

6.5   Further advances

6.5.1 Reasons for further advances

There are various reasons as to why a borrower might approach a lender for a **further advance**.

◆ The renewal of existing facilities – existing loan facilities may be due to expire, and the conduct and character of the borrower as well as the performance of the account, may justify the renewal of the facility for a further specified period.

◆ An increase in borrowing requirements, as a result of:

- the expansion of existing business, including increased turnover and new technologies;

- new investment activities, including new products and new markets.

◆ The availability of increased capital or collateral security, increasing the eligible loan amount.

◆ The borrower's need for a different interest rate structure, eg moving from a fixed to a floating rate of interest.

◆ The borrower's need for different loan products, eg a credit card borrower might request an overdraft.

♦ An improvement in borrower's credit rating might induce the borrower to seek enhanced facilities.

♦ A desire to consolidate loans.

6.5.2 Loan consolidation

Borrowers may approach the lender for **loan consolidation** in order to:

♦ save on interest and other costs by reducing overall borrowing – the lender might need to charge early redemption fees in order to safeguard against loss on account of early loan closures;

♦ lower monthly payments – a longer repayment period could facilitate reduction in outgoings for a borrower faced with a shortfall in liquidity;

♦ take advantage of increased asset values and increase loan amounts, eg homeowners in rising a house prices scenario;

♦ invest for the future in anticipation of increase in income levels, eg students.

In all cases, the lender needs to assess the viability of the loan and the ability of the borrower to meet repayment obligations.

Conclusion

The lending cycle consists of the credit granting process, the credit monitoring process and the credit recovery process. The credit granting process is the first stage in the lending cycle, and it consists, in turn, of a series of stages that include lead generation, loan application, loan evaluation and loan approval or rejection.

In order to originate good quality loans, lenders need to collect relevant and timely information about the prospective borrower and the activity for which the loan is sought. Information can be either 'hard' or 'soft', and the information needs to be gathered as well as interpreted.

Lenders use loan evaluation frameworks and checklists to evaluate a credit application. These canons of lending or loan criteria are expressed in the form of mnemonics for easy recall. Campari, CCCParts and Parser are examples of mnemonics used by a number of lending banks.

Credit scoring models and credit rating agencies enable lenders to determine who is eligible for a loan, what credit limit should be set and what interest rate should be charged.

Loan documentation incorporating relevant loan covenants is a very important stage in the lending process. An incorrectly or inadequately documented loan may not be enforceable. Lenders need to be able to obtain the relevant documents in a timely and appropriate manner.

Further reading

Gomez, C (2007) 'How Much Credit?' *Business Credit*, 2007. 109(3).

Panagiotou, George (2003) 'Bringing SWOT into Focus' *Business Strategy Review*, Summer 2003, Vol. 14 Issue 2.

Topic 6
Review questions, activities and case study

The following review questions, activities and case study are designed to increase your understanding of the material you have just studied.

◆ The **review questions** are designed so that you can check your understanding of this topic.

◆ Completion of the **activities** will give you further opportunity to research and understand, in more depth, the themes running through this topic.

◆ The **case study** encourages you to think further about the application of the content of this topic.

The answers to the questions and case study are provided at the end of these learning materials. Please note that the activities are open-ended and therefore a suitable 'answer' may not always be provided.

Review questions

?

1. What are the main components in the lending cycle?

2. What are the limitations of financial ratio analysis?

3. What are the advantages and disadvantages of credit scoring?

4. Why might a borrower approach a lender for further advances?

Activities

Activity 1

> Examine your own organisation's loan or other credit agreements and read the clauses. Are there any clauses that you had not noted before? What are the implications for the lender and borrower?
>
> If you have not entered into any loan agreement, collect or download a sample loan agreement form and scrutinise the document for any restrictive or affirmative clauses.

Activity 2

> Examine the change in the working capital ratio of BT over the period 2005–2007.
>
> Calculate the current ratio for the three years. Is the working capital positive or negative?
>
> | | £ in millions | | |
> | --- | --- | --- | --- |
> | | **31 Mar 2007** | **31 Mar 2006** | **31 Mar 2005** |
> | Cash and short-term investments | 1,105 | 2,399 | 4,496 |
> | Receivables | 3,380 | 2.916 | 2,423 |
> | Inventory | 133 | 124 | 106 |
> | Prepaid expenses | 922 | 686 | 423 |
> | Other current assets | 275 | 292 | 1,423 |
> | **Total current assets** | **5,815** | **6,417** | **9,321** |
> | Accounts payable | 3,717 | 3,466 | 2,921 |
> | Accrued expenses | 519 | 488 | 719 |
> | Short-term debt | 2,203 | 1,940 | 4,261 |
> | Other current liabilities | 3,178 | 3,586 | 4,203 |
> | **Total current liabilities** | **9,617** | **9,480** | **12,104** |

Case study

In *Titford Property v Cannon Street Acceptances Ltd* [1975] the loan agreement contained Clause 9, which specified that 'All moneys due by you, whether by way of capital or interest, shall be payable on demand and you shall have the right to repay all moneys due without notice.' A letter from the bank to the customer said: 'We have pleasure in advising you of the terms and conditions upon which we are prepared to provide an overdraft facility in the maximum sum of £248,000 for a period of 12 months to assist you in the purchase and development of the under mentioned freehold premises.' Thus the loan agreement and the facility letter contained contradictory clauses. It was held by Goff J that 'where a bank allows an overdraft for a fixed time for a specific purpose ...that time is binding on the bank', because otherwise, the customer will be in 'a disastrous position' of being unable to meet the liabilities that were incurred on the faith of the bank's promise to lend money.

In *Williams and Glyns Bank v Barnes* [1980], Gibson J stated that: 'Bankers ...regard repayability on demand as a universal or normal attribute of overdrafts, but there is nothing to suggest that they regard that attribute as overriding an agreement to the contrary. In this case, however, it was held that the bank had expressly reserved the right to withdraw the overdraft facilities at any time and that there was no contradictory statement upon which the customer could rely. Accordingly, the bank was entitled to immediate repayment once a proper demand had been made, because the bank had done nothing to remove its right for immediate repayment as had been done in *Titford.*

1   Which were the two items of loan documentation that were found to have contradictory clauses in *Titford*?

2   What was the contradiction in these documents?

3 What is the common conclusion about the nature of overdrafts reached by both of the cases mentioned above?

4 Why was the overdraft granted in *Titford* held not to be repayable on demand?

5 What is the lesson here for lenders?

Topic 7
Security – general

Learning outcomes

To be able to understand the advantages and disadvantages of taking appropriate security and the need to perfect security interest.

The learning areas include:

◆ the nature of security;

◆ the attributes of good security;

◆ the need to perfect security;

◆ clauses in charge forms;

◆ the advantages and disadvantages of obtaining security.

Introduction

To secure is to make safe. **Security** is what secures or guards a loan against default. **Securing a loan** protects against default and ensures that the loan is repaid in due course.

Security obtained by a lender is a claim on the borrower and on the asset that is secured, and provides a recourse that is available to a bank should the terms of the loan be breached by the borrower. In order for an asset to be converted into a security, it needs to be charged in favour of the lender. Procedures for charging an asset will vary depending upon the nature of the asset.

The **primary security** for a loan is the borrower. The lender lends because the borrower is considered to be creditworthy.

Creditworthiness is a lender's measure of likelihood that a borrower will meet debt obligations: it involves both the willingness and the ability of a borrower to repay a loan.

In addition to this primary security, the lender might wish to obtain assets owned by the borrower as safeguard in the event of default on a loan. A **clean or unsecured loan** is one that is not secured by any assets. The status of a loan is generally described by the amount of security available as back up. Thus a loan can be secured or unsecured or partly secured depending upon the availability and amount of the security.

Section 189(1) of the Consumer Credit Act 1974 defines a **security in relation to a consumer credit agreement** as 'a mortgage, charge, pledge, bond, debenture, indemnity, guarantee, bill, note or other right provided by the debtor or hirer, or at his request (express or implied), to secure the carrying out of the obligations of the debtor or hirer under the agreement'.

Security can be given either **directly** by the borrower, or by a **third party**, who is willing to guarantee the repayment of the debt.

7.1 The attributes of good security

The extent to which security is deemed to be desirable is determined by its value, as well as by factors relating to cost and administration (Willingham, 1997). The ideal security is one that:

- has adequate and stable value that is expected to rise over time
- easy to:
  - measure and monitor;
  - charge/take;
  - realise.

The **VMCR** mnemonic can be used to evaluate different types of security for desirability.

'Easy' refers to the extent to which it is cost effective and simple to carry out the relevant processes.

7.1.1 Valuable

Good security should have a stable value that is expected to increase over time. Generally the value of security in the form of land and property is considerable, and the value can be expected to rise over time, although crashes in property prices are also equally possible. A life policy, for example, may or may not be worth much when it has just commenced, but its value is likely to rise over time. The value of shares may or may not be considerable and can rise as well as fall.

7.1.2 Easy to measure and monitor

Some assets are comparatively simple to measure, while others are more difficult. Publicly quoted shares are easy to value by looking at a financial newspaper, but monitoring the value may be more time-consuming, because as they are liable to continuous fluctuations. Insurance policies can be instantly valued by asking the insurer. It may be more costly and difficult to value land, both in terms of time taken as well as the accuracy of estimates.

7.1.3 Easy to charge

Procedures for charging an asset vary with the nature of the asset. Insurance policies and shares are easy to charge, while the process of taking a charge on house property is more time consuming and expensive.

7.1.4 Easy to realise

> **Realisation** is the process of converting a secured asset into cash towards settlement of the debt due.

It is easy to sell shares and recoup the money on an insurance policy assigned in favour of the lender. It is more difficult to sell land and property quickly, and forced sales can lower the realisable value of these assets.

7.2 The perfection of security interest

An asset belonging to the borrower or a third party needs to be charged to the lender to enable the lender to use it as security. The **perfection** of security interest involves various steps that will need to be taken in order to ensure that the lender's interest in the security becomes enforceable. Failure to perfect a security interest properly can be fatal to the holder of the security interest (Wernick, 1991). Assets need to be charged in favour of the lender in order for the assets to become valid and enforceable security, and for the lender to have a valid and enforceable security interest in the assets acquired. Methods of perfecting security interest will vary with the type of security obtained, and some of these types are discussed in Topic 8.

> A **charge** is the process whereby an asset is converted by the lender to a security for the repayment of debt. A charge is a contractual agreement, which will specify:
>
> ◆   which assets are being taken as security;
>
> ◆   the circumstances in which the lender can dispose the assets;
>
> ◆   the circumstances in which the borrower can regain full control over the assets.

7.2.1 Forms of charge

Charges can take several forms.

♦ In a **legal charge**, title to the assets offered as security is transferred to the name of the lender. The lender assumes legal title to the asset, subject to the right of the borrower to have the assets retransferred when the conditions of the debt and its repayment are met.

♦ An **equitable charge** is a charge that arises according to natural justice, fairness or equity, notwithstanding any omission that might nullify a legal charge. For example, a legal charge that was never perfected or completed, but in relation to which the intention of the parties to the transaction was clear, has been held to mean that the asset being offered to the lender as security would result in an equitable charge. It has also been held that the mere deposit of title documents gave rise to an equitable charge. But this is no longer true in relation to land in England, although company shares can still be equitably mortgaged by deposit of share certificates.

The Court of Appeal in *United Bank of Kuwait v Sahib* [1996] held that the Law of Property (Miscellaneous Provisions) Act 1989 (which requires that any future disposition of land, including equitable charges, must be in writing) repealed the common law rules relating to the creation of equitable mortgages by deposit of title deeds. An equitable charge is not as effective as a legal charge: it will be extinguished by a bona fide purchaser for value who did not have notice of the mortgage and, even if valid, the lender will need to seek the court's approval for disposing the asset.

♦ A **fixed charge** confers a right on the lender to have recourse to a particular asset in the event of the debtor's default and is enforceable by the power of sale of the assets so charged.

♦ A **floating charge** is similar to a fixed charge once it crystallises. Crystallisation might take place upon the commencement of liquidation proceedings against the debtor. Prior to crystallisation, however, it 'floats' and covers assets such as stocks and goods over which the debtor continues to exercise physical control.

♦ In a **pledge**, sometimes called **bailment**, the borrower temporarily gives possession of property to the lender to provide assurance that the debt will be repaid. Pledges were used in old-fashioned 'lock and key' advances, under which the lender retained goods under lock and key, and took delivery of, and released, goods as and when required by the borrower to meet day-to-day operating requirements. They are still widely used by pawnbrokers, who continue to remain as a regulated credit industry. A pledge does not confer a right to sale or disposal of property.

♦ A **lien** is a right to retain physical possession of tangible assets as security for underlying obligations. In *Brandao v Barnett* [1846] it was held that a **banker's lien** is a general lien on all instruments, such as cheques and bills, deposited with the bank by a customer, unless there was an express or implied contract to the contrary.

7.3 The terms and conditions of charging security

The lender needs to make clear the terms and conditions under which a loan is extended to the borrower in such a way as to avoid any ambiguity in the interpretation of the clauses. There are some lenders who merely state on the application forms that 'terms and conditions are available on request' and do not take care to make these clear to the borrower; such practices are fraught with danger and need to be avoided.

Clauses in the charge forms will be usually drawn up in consultation with legal practitioners, so that they comply with legal and regulatory requirements and facilitate the recovery of payments as and when they fall due. Lenders need to draw up the terms and conditions carefully, so that every eventuality is anticipated and the security becomes enforceable. Lenders also need to ensure that their terms and conditions do not violate the provisions of the Unfair Contract Terms Act 1977, because as any perceived contraventions might nullify the value of the security in the eyes of the law.

Some of the standard clauses in loan agreements and charge forms are:

- the all moneys clause;

- the continuing security clause;

- the after acquired clause;

- the repayment on demand clause;

- the conclusive evidence clause;

- the successor clause.

The **all moneys clause** prevents the release of title until all sums due have been paid. For example, a lender who has extended a mortgage against the security of a house property will be able to retain title to the property until the borrower has repaid all dues including any credit card and unsecured overdraft borrowings that might have been granted to the borrower by the same lender. The mortgage of house property will thus extend to all debts of the borrower with the lender. In order to reiterate the right to the repayment of 'all moneys' the agreement will also usually include a further clause specifically excluding the operation of s 93 of the Law of Property Act 1925, which restricts the consolidation of mortgages. These clauses will ensure that the borrower does not seek the release of some, or part, of the security on a partial repayment of the loan.

A **continuing security clause** indicates that the security continues to remain in force notwithstanding any interim payments made in satisfaction of the debt until such time as the liabilities are discharged in full, and that the security will not prejudice, or be prejudiced by, any other security that might be held by the lender. The effect of this clause is to prevent the rule in *Clayton's Case* from becoming operative. The borrower will be prevented from arguing that subsequent deposits had the effect of cancelling earlier debts.

An **after acquired clause** covers subsequent acquisitions of assets by the borrower and includes such assets as collateral security for an existing loan. For example, a borrower whose property is mortgaged under a loan with an after acquired clause may purchase adjacent land for further development, but will be unable to raise a new mortgage, because the after-acquired land is captured as security for the existing mortgage.

A **repayment on demand clause** gives a lender the right of repayment on demand. The inclusion of a repayment on demand clause will exclude the delays envisaged by s 103 of the Law of Property Act 1925, which prescribes certain minimum time periods for exercising the right to realise collateral security. By using this clause lenders are able to reserve for themselves the right to proceed more quickly with the sale of charged property.

A **conclusive evidence clause** states that something is not open or liable to be questioned or challenged. For example, a document signed by the lender may be deemed to be conclusive evidence, as between the lender and guarantor, of the amount of the liability under the guarantee or mortgage. A conclusive evidence clause provides the lender with an expeditious way of proving the borrower's liability, particularly in circumstances in which the transactions are complex and proving each one will take much time and effort.

The validity of conclusive evidence clauses has been upheld by courts on many occasions. In *Bache & Co (London) Ltd v Banque Vernes et Commerciale De Paris SA* [1973], Lord Denning held that 'this commercial practice [of inserting "conclusive evidence" clauses] is only acceptable because the bankers or brokers who insert them are known to be honest and reliable men of business who are most unlikely to make a mistake. Their standing is so high that their word is to be trusted. So much so that a notice of default given by a bank or a broker must be honoured.'

In *Dobbs v National Bank of Australasia Ltd* [1935] the clause provided that a certificate signed by the manager or acting manager of the office at which the debtor's account was kept should be conclusive evidence of his indebtedness at the date of the certificate.

A **successor clause** makes an agreement binding upon the parties, 'their successors, and assigns', regardless of whether the nature of such successors is changed by reorganisation, acquisition or reconstitution. For example, the use of the clause will ensure that change of Bradford and Bingley from a building society to a bank will not adversely affect the status of a loan extended to a borrower when it was a building society.

Activity

Activity 1

> Read the clauses in any charge form that you might have executed (eg in relation to a mortgage). Identify the clauses discussed above within the charge form.

7.4 Independent legal advice

It is good practice for a lender to ask the borrower(s) to obtain independent legal advice prior to obtaining their signature(s) on the charge forms. In order to be independent, legal advice needs to come from a lawyer not associated with the other contracting party – the lender, in this case. A **Certificate of Independent Legal Advice** (**CILA**) is a document that attests that a person has received legal advice on a proposed contract from an independent lawyer not associated with the other contracting party. When a borrower receives independent legal advice about a loan contract, they will be precluded from later claiming that they were not aware of what they were signing or the consequences of what they were signing.

Between two parties to a contract, one party might be deemed to be in a stronger position that might give rise to a situation in which the weaker party claims that the stronger party exerted an undue influence to the detriment of the weaker party. Between a banker and a borrower, the borrower will be the weaker party.

In *Allcard v Skinner* [1887] it was held that where one party has obtained benefit by exercising undue influence, the contract will be set aside. Allegations of undue influence have been successfully upheld in courts in situations where a wife had guaranteed loans extended to the husband, or in which an elderly father had guaranteed advances to the son. It is therefore extremely important that lenders protect themselves against the charge of undue influence by insisting that the borrower/guarantor seeks and obtains independent legal advice before signing any charge form.

Recent cases concerning undue influence include *Barclays Bank plc v O'Brien* [1994] and *Royal Bank of Scotland plc v Etridge* [2001] the court acknowledged that the relationship between the debtor and the surety as man and wife was such that there may be an issue of undue influence. The lender should have been put on inquiry when taking the security and should have taken reasonable steps to ensure that the wife's agreement to stand surety has been properly obtained. If the lender cannot show that reasonable steps had been taken, the security cannot be enforced. Since *Etridge*, it is no longer sufficient to seek a certificate from a solicitor that the wife was independently advised of the risks she was taking when granting the security. New guidelines require a number of steps to be taken, including direct communication between the lender and the wife/guarantor. Lenders need to set up appropriate internal procedures to ensure compliance with the law and to seek legal advice as appropriate.

7.5 The desirability of taking collateral security

Lenders need to be aware that collateral security has advantages as well as disadvantages.

7.5.1 Advantages of taking collateral security

◆ Security reduces the risk caused by asymmetry of information and serves as an incentive for borrowers to repay, thus reducing loan losses and increasing profits. (Asymmetry of information occurs when one party has more, or better, information than the other party.)

◆ As security lowers credit default risk, the lender is able to charge lower interest, thereby easing the cost of capital for business and consumers. A quick comparison of interest rates charged for secured mortgages and unsecured loans will make this obvious.

◆ Security enables lenders to extend finance to certain high risk borrowers who might otherwise not be eligible. Lenders should be aware, however, that the provision of security does not make a bad proposition good.

7.5.2 Disadvantages of taking collateral security

♦ Taking security is time-consuming and often involves complicated paperwork, eg regulated agreements under the Consumer Credit Act 1974.

♦ Taking security involves costs and these costs are generally passed on to the borrower raising their overall borrowing costs. In some cases such as property these costs can be quite high.

♦ The **retention of title (ROT) clause**, sometimes also known as the Romalpa caluse after the case of *Aluminium Industrie Vaassen BV v Romalpa Aluminium Ltd* [1976], expressly provides for the retention of legal title to any goods that a seller might have handed over to the buyer until the goods are paid for. Thus some of the goods that a lender might consider as being available as security under a floating charge might, in fact, be beyond the reach of the lender, because the title to those goods might continue to vest with the seller (see section 8.5.3).

♦ Problems might arise if it is difficult to identify the precise assets that are charged to the lender, particularly if they are mixed up with others that are not.

♦ Taking security does not preclude losses. Legal and other reasons might reduce or remove the security that was deemed to be available in the case of borrower default. Undue influence, non est factum, mispresentation and misapprehension, for example, have been cited by borrowers and guarantors to escape liability. Lenders who have sued borrowers for their security are known to have lost, incurring additional legal costs in the process.

♦ There might be other circumstances under which the lender loses more money as a result of obtaining security. For example, the liability of a lender, who has financed a borrower, who has been found guilty of environmental pollution, might be unlimited if the borrower is unable to meet the costs and goes into insolvency.

Conclusion

The primary security for a loan is the borrower. The lender lends because the borrower is considered to be creditworthy. In addition to this primary security, the lender might wish to obtain assets owned by the borrower as safeguard in the event of default on a loan. Assets so obtained as security for a loan are known as collateral security or just collateral, as they are obtained as a back-up in the event of the unwillingness or inability of a borrower to repay a loan.

The extent to which security is deemed to be desirable determined by its value as well as factors relating to cost and administration. The ideal security is one which has adequate and stable value that is expected to rise over time, and which is easy to measure and monitor, easy to take and easy to realise.

Lenders need to be aware that collateral security has advantages as well as disadvantages. There might be circumstances where the lender might be better off by not obtaining security.

Further reading

Lucas, D. (2007) 'It's OK, we are secured – fact or fiction?' *ifs* Lead tutor article.

Topic 7

Review questions and case study

The following review questions and case study are designed to increase your understanding of the material you have just studied.

◆ The **review questions** are designed so that you can check your understanding of this topic.

◆ The **case study** encourages you to think further about the application of the content of this topic.

The answers to the questions and case study are provided at the end of these learning materials.

Review questions

1. Why do lenders take security?

2. What are the attributes of good security?

3. Why do lenders recommend that guarantors and borrowers should seek independent legal advice?

4. Examine the clauses that are incorporated in bank charge forms.

5.   What are the disadvantages of taking security?

Case study – *West Bromwich Building Society v Wilkinson* [2005]

Mark and Lynne Wilkinson bought a house in Norfolk in October 1988 with the help of a loan from the West Bromwich Building Society, which lent them a sum of £35,895 against the mortgage of the property. The loan was repayable with interest by monthly instalments of about £480.

The Wilkinsons defaulted almost immediately, after paying only two instalments in 1989. On 25 July 1989 the building society obtained an order for possession, which was executed on 9 October 1989. The property market was, at that time, in decline and it was some time before the building society could negotiate a sale. More than a year later, on 14 November 1990, it sold the house for £34,000, leaving a shortfall of £23,921.92, representing arrears of interest and other charges.

After giving up possession, the Wilkinsons moved into other accommodation. They subsequently separated and lived at different addresses. The building society did not contact them for over 12 years. In November 2002, however, it served the Wilkinsons with a claim for £46,865.99 and costs, which represented the shortfall on the sale in 1990 with accumulated interest. The Wilkinsons said that the building society's claim was barred by s 20(1) of the Limitation Act 1980, a claim that was contested by the building society.

The Limitation Act 1980 provides timescales within which action may be taken for breaches of the law. For example, it provides that breaches of an ordinary contract are actionable for six years after the event, while breaches of a deed, such as a mortgage deed in this case, are actionable for 12 years after the event: 'No action shall be brought to recover…any principal sum of money secured by a mortgage or other charge on property after the expiration of 12 years from the date on which the right to receive the money accrued.'

In 2005, the House of Lords held that that the building society's claim in this action, which was commenced on 12 November 2002, was statute barred. The default by the borrowers in paying a monthly instalment had the result of making the entire loan outstandings become repayable and entitled the Building Society to sell the house. The lender had given a notice in writing requiring payment 'forthwith of the moneys hereby secured' and therefore the mortgage money outstanding had become due and payable by Mr and Mrs Wilkinson one month after they had made default in paying a monthly instalment. For the purposes of the Limitation Act 1980, time had begun to run well before 9 October 1989 when the Society took possession of the house with a view to its sale. Therefore the appeal by the building society was dismissed.

1 What was the security obtained by West Bromwich Building Society when it extended a loan to Mark and Lynne Wilkinson in October 1988?

2 What are the possible reasons for the shortfall in the sale proceeds of the collateral security in relation to the loan granted.

3 Why is the Limitation Act 1980 so named?

4 What is the limitation period for a mortgage deed?

5 Why was the case considered to be statute barred?

6 What are the lessons here for lenders?

Topic 8
Security – specific forms

> **Learning outcomes** Being able to apply the principles of security to various forms of assets.
>
> The learning areas include an examination of the following assets as forms of security:
>
> ◆ land and property;
>
> ◆ stocks and shares;
>
> ◆ life policies;
>
> ◆ guarantees;
>
> ◆ debentures incorporating fixed and floating charges.

Introduction

Security can take the following forms:

◆ **proprietary security**, such as commercial or residential land and property. In the case of proprietory security, the lender does not take possession of the asset and the borrower is able to continue to make use of it;

◆ **possessory security** in relation to which the lender is able to take possession of the assets, eg assets such as accounts receivable/book debts and goods/stock lying in the borrower's premises, although, in practical terms, physical possession has to be retained by the chargor;

◆ **intangible security** over assets such as intellectual property and licence fees payable for the use of software, etc;

◆ **financial instruments**, such as shares and bonds;

◆ **insurance policies**;

◆ **third-party security** such as guarantees with or without security owned by the third party;

◆ **choses in action**, or security of which the lender is not in possession, but which can be demanded in law. Examples are rights of set off over deposits and credit balances held either with a lender or with other institutions over which the lender can exercise a right;

◆ **debentures**, which include fixed and/or floating charges.

Some of these forms of security are examined below.

8.1 Land and property

8.1.1 Nature and types

> The definition of **land** includes any buildings situated upon the land, particularly if parts of buildings at different levels are in different ownership, as is the case in relation to flats.

The Land Registration Act 2002 and Land Registration Rules 2003 came into force in the UK on 13 October 2003. The new Act and rules govern the role and practice of HM Land Registry, and provide a more complete picture of a **title to land** and the **rights** and **interests** affecting it. They also introduced a framework for the development of **electronic conveyancing**.

The Land Registry records the ownership rights of freehold properties as well as leasehold properties for which the lease has been granted for a term of more than seven years, and guarantees title to registered estates and interests in land.

8.1.1.1 Legal estates in land

> **Registered land** is land that has been registered with HM Land Registry (HMLR). The land certificate evidences title to registered land.

The certificate bears its own number, which identifies the property in the record at HMLR. The land certificate contains copies of the three registers held at HMLR, which are:

1. the property register containing a brief description of the property, including number and stating whether it is freehold or leasehold;

2. the proprietorship register containing name(s) of owner(s) and title held, ie absolute, good leasehold, possessory or qualified;

3. the charges register showing any other interests in the property, ie mortgages, restrictive covenants, notices under the Matrimonial Homes Act, etc.

> **Unregistered land** is land that has not yet been registered with the Land Registry. Title to unregistered land is evidenced by title deeds. These are documents of past title interests and charges and should form an unbroken chain of title to the current owner.

The land charges department of the Land Registry maintains a computerised record relating to the charges on unregistered land. The registered purchaser's interest gets priority over all other interests. In *Whittington v Whittington, National Westminster Intervening* [1978], it was held that a lender's charge registered subsequent to a court order for a wife's action for the property of her husband had priority, because the wife's action had not been registered.

Freehold is a perpetual right in relation to which there is no limit of time to hold the property. **Absolute freehold title** evidences absolute title in freehold property subject to entries on the register and unregistered or overriding interests. In **possessory freehold title** there is no documentary evidence of title and the title depends on adverse possession. (**Adverse possession** allows a person to obtain title to land by being in possession of the land for a specified period of time). It conveys no guarantee of title at the time of registration, but it can be upgraded into absolute title after being in possession as proprietor for 12 years. **Qualified freehold title** is subject to a fundamental defect.

Leasehold estates are subject to specific time limits. **Absolute leasehold title** is leasehold similar to absolute freehold, but is also subject to covenants in the lease. **Good leasehold title** is leasehold that is similar to absolute leasehold, but the right of the landlord to grant the lease is not guaranteed. **Possessory leasehold** title is leasehold similar to **possessory freehold** and **qualified leasehold** title is leasehold similar to qualified freehold.

A **legal mortgage** is 'a charge by deed' under which the lender gains sufficient rights over the property so as to enforce the security, such as to take possession of the property or to sell it. A legal mortgage will be recorded by the Land Registry. According to s 29 of the Land Registration Act 2002, a person acquiring a legal estate for valuable consideration as owner takes it subject to any notices on the charges register, any unregistered interests that override (formerly known as 'overriding interests') and, if the estate is a lease, any burdens or covenants that are incidental to the lease. A person such as a wife who is in actual occupation of a property may acquire an overriding interest in the property even if such interest is not registered (*Williams and Glyn's Bank Ltd v Boland* [1981]. Since *Boland*, lenders take steps to ensure that the occupants of a property being mortgaged give their informed consent to the mortgage in writing.

In an **equitable mortgage** the mortgagee obtains only an equitable interest. This may occur because the mortgagor has only an equitable interest or because all of the formalities required for a legal mortgage have not been completed.

Both legal and equitable mortgages are non-possessory security interests. Usually, the mortgagor will remain in possession of the mortgaged asset.

A prudent lender will obtain security that has absolute title, and reject other types of property, ie qualified or possessory title in which title is not absolute.

8.1.2   The advantages of land and property as security

◆ Land is usually the most valuable asset that is available to a lender as security. Values tend to rise faster than inflation.

◆ Clear proprietory title can be obtained for registered land and it will be guaranteed by the Land Registry, subject to any defects, covenants, etc. The Land Registry is actively encouraging owners of unregistered land to register their properties.

◆ Land is usually the main asset of a borrower and serves as a powerful incentive to make repayment of debts secured by the asset.

◆ Because the security of land will be expected to reduce considerably the risk of default, the lender is able to charge lower interest.

◆ There is always a demand for land, as its supply is fixed.

◆ The value of domestic property is fairly easy to estimate by means of comparison with the sale prices of nearby properties in the neighbourhood. Sale prices of neighbouring properties are readily available from the Land Registry and also from other dedicated websites.

◆ For registered land, the title documentation is fairly simple, there being only one document of title: the land certificate.

8.1.3 The disadvantages of land and property as security

◆ There have been periods during which property prices have consistently fallen, wiping out any available equity and giving rise to the situation of **negative equity**, ie where the loan amount exceeds the value of the security. It is therefore important for lenders to ensure that there is an adequate margin between the value of the security and the amount of the loan.

◆ Taking a security interest in land is relatively time consuming and involves complex documentation that will need to be examined by qualified solicitors or conveyancers.

◆ The costs of securing land are high. Valuation, legal and other costs will need to be incurred, but these will generally be passed on to the borrower.

◆ Realisation may be a slow process.

◆ The valuation of factory or other industrial premises may be particularly difficult. Valuation may not be accurate. Each property is different and comparisons with other properties may not be appropriate.

◆ Valuation may prove to be inaccurate, and the lender may not be able to hold professional valuers responsible for losses.

◆ For unregistered land, the title documentation is fairly complex, because all prior documentation needs to be verified and a 15-year chain of title must be established.

◆ In certain circumstances, the creation of a second mortgage will have legal implications for the first mortgagee, as indicated below. Upon receipt of notice of a second charge, a running account secured by the property must be ruled off to avoid the effects of the rule in *Clayton's Case*.

8.1.4 Second mortgages

A **second mortgage** is a security interest created in a property that is already subject to a first legal charge. The claim of the second mortgagee will rank subsequent to that of the first mortgagee, but above any subsequent mortgagees such as a third mortgagee. In the event of sale of the property, the sale proceeds will be first used to pay off the outstanding first mortgage and the balance applied to subsequent charges in order of registration at the Land Registry.

Second mortgages allow borrowers the opportunity to raise capital or to release the equity in their property without having to remortgage, particularly when property prices are rising and when available equity rises correspondingly. As long as sufficient equity is available in the property, a lender may be willing to extend advances against a second charge on the property.

In certain circumstances, a second mortgagee may find the security interest diluted if the first mortgagee is able to 'tack' advances granted subsequent to the second mortgage onto the original first mortgage, thus gaining priority over the second mortgagee in respect of subsequent advances.

Tacking may arise in respect of competing priorities between two or more security interests over the same asset. It is the adding on of a loan given by a lender at a subsequent period to a loan granted earlier, so as to prevent an intermediate lender from gaining priority over the first lender in respect to the further advances granted by the first lender.

The Law of Property Act 1925 abolished tacking, except as expressly allowed by s 94 of the Act, which permits tacking if the first mortgage 'imposes an obligation' on the first lender 'to make such further advances'. Because lenders usually do not commit themselves to such further advances, however, the applicability of tacking in the case of second mortgages will be rare.

To illustrate, lender A extends a loan against a first mortgage of property. Lender B extends a second loan against a second mortgage of the same property. Lender B's claim will rank second to Lender A, but prior to all subsequent mortgages. If Lender A then extends further advances against the same property, lender A's claim in regard to such further advances will rank subsequent to that of Lender B, unless Lender A can prove that the first loan granted carried an obligation to grant such further advances.

When taking a charge over registered land a search must first be made at HM Land Registry and this search effectively freezes the register and gives the searcher 30 days to register their interest. The charge will always be subservient to any prior charge registered, whether legal or equitable, and the mortgagee cannot obtain precedence over prior interests.

Before a subsequent charge is registered the registrar will write to all prior mortgagees to obtain their consent to the creation of the new charge. This is considered effective notice to prior mortgagees but, in practice, the subsequent mortgagee will always serve notice of their interest to parties with a prior interest. Priority is determined by date of registration, not date of charge.

With unregistered land, if the first mortgagee holds the deeds then it is not possible to register a charge at HM Land Charges Register. Possession of the deeds by the first mortgagee is sufficient notice to the world of their charge. Any subsequent mortgagees will register their interest at HM Land Charges Registry as a 'puisne mortgage', ie a mortgage not protected by deposit of the title deeds. As with registered land priority is determined by date of registration of charge not date of creation.

To sum up, land is valuable and the value generally rises over time, but it is relatively slow or difficult to value, charge and realise.

8.2   Life assurance policies

Insurance can be defined as protection against risks of financial loss, against the possibility that the insured event may take place. (Kapoor et al, 2004). **Assurance** is the provision of financial benefit following an event that is certain to occur, ie death or maturity.

An **insurance company** or **insurer** is a financial intermediary that, for a price, promises to pay specified sums contingent on future events. The insurer provides protection in the form of a policy to cover a person's life or property or liability. Insurance is a legally binding contract between the insured and the insurer, ie the policy holder and the insurance company. In return for the payment of premiums the insurer indemnifies the insured against certain insurable risks.

Premium is the price of insurance paid in a lump sum or in instalments over a period of time.

The premiums paid by members into the pool are calculated by the insurance company's loss prediction system. Relevant statute law includes the Life Assurance Act 1774, the Policies of Assurance Act 1867, the Insurance Companies Act 1980 and the Financial Services and Markets Act 2000.

8.2.1   Principles of insurance

The lender needs to be aware of the key principles of insurance while using insurance as a means of mitigating risk.

♦ **The contract of indemnity**: the insurers agree to compensate in the event of loss such that the insured is left substantially in the same position financially after the loss, as if the loss had not taken place at all. The insured cannot profit from a loss or damage.

♦ **The duty of utmost good faith** (*uberrimae fidae*): All material facts about an insured risk must be disclosed to the insurers at the time of completing the proposal form or subsequently, if the facts change. The relationship between insurer and insured is characterised by a considerable asymmetry of information. Misrepresentation of material facts will render the insurance void.

♦ **The requirement of insurable interest**: the insured must be so situated in relation to the matter insured as to benefit by its existence and sustain loss from its destruction – that is the insured must have an *actual pecuniary interest* in the subject matter of the insurance. Examples of insurable interests include:

  – the proposer's own life;

  – the life of a partner;

  – the life of any children on whom the proposer is dependent;

  – a creditor on the life of a debtor.

Insurable interest must be present at the time of entering into the contract; this interest can subside but the claim will remain valid. The opposite occurs with fire insurance where interest must be present at the time of the claim.

8.2.2 Nature and types

Life assurance is a form of personal insurance, whereas property insurance is a form of general insurance. Thus insurance can be divided under two major categories:

◆ personal insurance;

◆ general insurance.

Personal insurance provides personal protection and includes life insurance, health insurance, employment insurance and other related forms of insurance.

General insurance covers against the risk that an event might happen and includes fire and accident insurance for property, motor vehicles, personal belongsing, etc.

Life assurance pays a lump sum or the 'sum assured' to dependants on death during the life of the policy in return for payment of premiums to an insurance company, usually monthly or annually. Life insurance premiums will vary depending upon the sum assured, the length or term of the policy plus individual lifestyle factors such as age, occupation, gender, state of health, whether the insured is a smoker, etc.

Life insurance can cover a number of personal contingencies and includes the following types.

◆ **Term life insurance** provides life cover for a fixed term, pays a lump sum on death during the term of the cover, and could be decreasing term insurance or level term insurance. While these policies are often used to cover a mortgage, they have no cash value or surrender value and are therefore unsuitable as security.

◆ **Whole-of-life insurance** pays a lump sum on death. Payout is certain, because death is inevitable, and lenders are willing to take a policy that has sufficient surrender value as security.

8.2.3 The use of insurance in lending

The lender can make use of insurance in a variety of ways in order to mitigate credit risk.

◆ The security itself may be insured. Where a loan is given in order to enable the borrower to purchase certain assets such as land, buildings, cars, etc, these assets are insured so that any damage to them is covered. The value of the security is thereby protected against unforeseen loss.

◆ Insurance may be taken out by the borrower in addition to or in lieu of security. The borrower arranges for insurance either of their own volition or at the behest of the lender in order to safeguard the lender against potential losses. For example, the lender might require a borrower to take out life assurance or disability insurance that will pay out to the creditor if the borrower were to suffer an accident or die before the debt is repaid. A mortgage protection policy, for example, pays out if a mortgagor is in default.

◆ Insurance policies can, in themselves, constitute security against which loans are extended. For example, a life assurance policy on which premiums have been paid for a number of years could have accumulated a considerable surrender value and this can serve as security for a loan. This use of life assurance policies in lending is considered in greater detail next.

Assignment is giving the benefit of the insurance policy to somebody else, in this case the lender. The assigment must be witnessed and signed in accordance with the Policies of Assurance Act 1867.

8.2.4 The advantages of assurance policies as security

♦ Life assurance policies are very easy to value. The surrender value of the policy will be readily available from the insurance company on request.

♦ The value increases provided that the insurance premium is paid as stipulated.

♦ The procedure for taking a charge is relatively simple and easy. A legal assignment involves sending an assignment form signed by the borrower to the insurance company, which will notify the lender of having noted the assignment. In *Myers v United Guarantee and Life Assurance Co* [1855], it was held that an equitable assignment may be made orally, or by memorandum, or by deposit of the policy with the intent to create a security.

♦ Realisation is relatively straightforward, simply requiring the surrender of the policy.

♦ In the event of the borrower's death, the insurer's payout will go towards liquidating a part, or whole, of the debt.

♦ A legal mortgage over a policy has the following advantages:

 – it will take priority provided that the lender retains the policy and that the insurer confirms that there are no other known charges;

 – at the request of the lender, the insurer is bound to note the lender's security interest in the policy;

 – the lender will not require the agreement of the beneficiary of the policy to surrender or claim maturity proceeds.

8.2.5 The disadvantages of insurance policies as security

♦ Life policies are not always available as security for a number of reasons.

♦ The beneficiary, who will be signing the change form, should be the person receiving the moneys upon the death of the life assured and also the owner of the policy.

If the beneficiary is not the principal debtor, then it will be a third-party security. If this is the case, you should ensure that the parties are independently advised and that the standard clauses have been explained to them by the bank in order to avoid a claim of undue influence.

If the policy is issued under s 11(2) of the Married Women's Property Act 1882, the beneficiaries could be described as 'my wife and children'. In *Re Browne's Policy* [1903] it was held that this created a trust in favour of the named beneficiaries alive at the time of the claim. The policy could specifically name the beneficiaries, eg 'my wife Ann and my children Mark and John'. For these policies the charge form of legal assignment must be signed by both the proposer and all beneficiaries. To be fully effective, the beneficiaries must be named with certainty and have full contractual capacity.

◆ New policies have either no or inadequate surrender value.

◆ The insurer is able to set off an earlier claim with the assured prior to receipt of notice of assignment.

◆ Because a contract for life insurance is a contract of utmost good faith, any non-disclosure of material facts will render the policy void. Material facts will influence the premium amount to be determined and the decision as to whether the risk should be assumed. In *London Assurance v Mansel* [1879] non-disclosure of the refusal of life insurance by a number of other insurers was deemed to be a material fact. In *Lindenau v Desborough* [1828] non-disclosure of doubts about the mental health of the assured was deemed to be a material fact, because a mentally ill person might be more prone to suicide.

◆ Equitable mortgages of life policies have a number of disadvantages:

  – they are subject to prior equities;

  – the insurance company is not obliged to take note of any notice received from a lender;

  – the beneficiary of the policy needs to authorise the insurance company to pay the proceeds to the lender. If the beneficiary does not co-operate, the lender will have to go to court to realise the proceeds.

For these reasons, equitable charges over life policies are rarely used.

To sum up, life policies are easy to take, easy to monitor and relatively easy to realise, but not all policies will have sufficient value to be of use as security.

8.3   Stocks and shares

8.3.1   Nature and types

A share of **stock** represents a unit of ownership in the issuing company. There are two main types of stock: common and preferred.

Common stock, or **ordinary shares**, confer on the owner voting rights, the right of a share in the earnings and a claim on the company assets in the event of liquidation. Ordinary shareholders are the ultimate risk-bearers of a company and are hence known as **equity holders**, and ordinary shares are known as **equity**.

Preferred stock, or **preference shares**, generally do not have voting rights, but have a prior claim on assets and earnings over ordinary shares. Preferred stock holders receive dividends before ordinary shareholders and have priority over ordinary shareholders in the event of company insolvency. Preferred stock is more like bonds or loans than shares, because the return is fixed and whatever profits remain go to the ordinary shareholders.

The market value of a share is influenced by a number of factors, such as its financial condition, its growth potential, and its earnings and dividend record, as well as external factors such as the general state of the economy.

The main categories of common stock have been described as follows.

- **Blue-chip stocks** are high quality stocks issued by well-established companies with many years of proven success and earnings growth. They tend to be a relatively safe form of security.

- **Income stocks** yield a higher than average dividend income. The value of such stocks is not likely to appreciate much, because a high proportion of the earnings are paid out as dividends.

- **Growth stocks** are expected to grow rapidly. Because profits are ploughed back into the business, the dividend yield may be low. The lender may find the value of the stock rising quickly if the company performs as expected.

- **Speculative stocks** may be issued by little-known or newly-formed companies, or they may be 'penny stocks' which have little or no value. This category will not be considered to be suitable security by lenders.

Common types of share include the following.

- **Partly-paid shares** are shares that have not yet been fully paid up, and on which the company has a right to call for further or remaining payment.

- **Foreign shares** are shares in companies registered abroad and may or may not be expressed in foreign currency.

- **Shares in private companies** are not publicly quoted in the stock exchange and are not subject to the rigorous listing requirements of publicly quoted companies.

While there are a number of other types of securities available to a lender as security, the discussion here is limited to stocks and shares.

8.3.2 The advantages of stocks and shares as security

- The value of stocks and shares tends to grow over time. Growth stocks, for example, which pay low or no dividends and reinvest company profits, can rise fairly quickly in value. As a whole, the stock market has had an upward trend in values, with years of gain generally outnumbering those of decline (but see section 8.3.3).

- Monitoring the value of stocks and shares traded on major exchanges is simple, because prices are readily available via electronic screens and the financial press.

- It is comparatively easy to take a charge over this form of security. In *Harrold v Plenty* [1909] the mere deposit of share certificates, with the intent that it was to be held as security, was construed as having created an equitable charge for the lender. If the share certificate is deposited, with a signed memorandum of deposit under seal containing an irrevocable attorney in favour of the mortgagee, then the bank can sell the shares without sanction of courts or consent of the mortgagor. An equitable mortgage has been taken but the bank can sell under the power of attorney provided by the customer. In practice, in respect of each share holding, a signed, undated, stock transfer form would be taken and held with the memorandum of deposit.

  A legal charge created by transfer of shares in the lender's name gives complete control over the shares and enables the lender to sell the shares in the event of loan default. Lenders usually keep shares in nominee accounts and have full power of sale should default occur. Provided that the lender is not aware of any defects in the title to the shares, a legal charge gives the lender priority over any prior equitable rights.

◆ Realisation is fairly straightforward. Stocks traded on major exchanges can be bought and sold quickly and easily at readily ascertainable prices, and are therefore highly liquid.

8.3.3 The disadvantages of stocks and shares as security

◆ There is a risk that the value may fall over time: companies may fail, stock prices may drop and the value of the security may disappear. Even if shares are generally performing well, shares in a single company may perform badly and the lender may see the value of the security diluted over time.

◆ Shares fluctuate in value and continuous monitoring of the share price will be required. The stock market can be very volatile and prone to sudden withdrawals of large amounts of funds by big players such as insurance, pension funds and international banks.

◆ The value of shares may be inflated owing to fraud or overstatement of values in the company books.

◆ The value of shares will be dependent upon a number of external factors over which neither the lender nor the borrower have much control, eg the condition of the market, the state of the company, speculative bids, ratings by credit rating agencies, etc.

◆ Unlike land and property, in relation to which lenders are happy to lend up to 90% or more of the value of the asset, a margin of at least 25-30% is recommended in the case of shares (Willingham, 1997).

◆ While lenders may like to take a number of different shares as security rather than shares in a single company in order to diversify risk, such diversification will come at the cost of increased paperwork.

◆ The forced sale of a large stake in a company may depress the share price. Realisation will also involve costs such as brokerage commissions.

◆ The restructuring of company shares may cause problems for the lender. For example, in the event of a **rights issue**, existing shareholders have the right to buy a specified number of new shares from the company at a specified (lower) price within a specified time. The right to buy new shares in the company may be rejected, accepted in full or accepted in part by each shareholder. Rights are often transferable, allowing the holder to sell them on the open market. Rights can be **renounceable** (sold separately from the share to other investors) or **non-renounceable** (shareholders must either take up the rights or let them lapse). Once the rights have lapsed, they no longer have any value. A lender who does not have a legal charge over shares may not be aware of the rights issue at all and the value of the shares that they hold as security will be reduced whether the borrower exercises the rights and acquires new shares that are not deposited as further security, or if the rights are allowed to lapse. Similarly, a **bonus issue**, which involves the issue of additional shares at no extra cost, has the effect of lowering the market value of existing shares while increasing the overall number of shares on issue. Lenders who do not have a legal charge over shares may not be aware of the bonus issue and the value of the shares they hold as security will be reduced if the borrower does not deposit the additional bonus shares received as additional security.

♦ If the share transfer form or letter are forged, the lender will lose the right to the shares taken as security. In *Sheffield Corporation v Barclay* [1905] the signature of one of the transferors was forged the company had to reimburse the person whose signature was forged, and the bank had to reimburse the company for the implied wrongful warranty that the signature was genuine.

♦ Many companies require that their directors hold a certain minimum number of company shares to qualify them as directors. If the director were to execute a legal charge to a lender for transfer of such 'qualification' shares, that would make them lose the qualification to be a director on the board of the company.

♦ In some countries, such as the USA, there are regulations that stipulate a high margin or low loan to value (LTV) ratio to prevent speculation in stocks using borrowed funds.

♦ The stock market is growing in complexity and opacity. Market turbulence can wipe out the value of a lender's security within a very short time.

♦ Unquoted shares will pose special problems. There may be restrictions on ownership and consequently, if a need for sale arises, it may be difficult to find investors willing to buy. Unlike quoted shares, there will be difficulty in ascertaining current prices. Even if valuation is made by a comparison with similar quoted companies, the absence of ready quotations and valuation will deter potential buyers.

♦ Foreign shares may be subject to foreign law as well as subject to currency risk due to fluctuation in the exchange rate.

♦ Partly paid shares will involve further payments by the shareholders as and when the company makes a **call** for such payments. There is a chance that such shares will become worthless if the **call money** is not paid up on time. If the lender has a legal charge on such shares, the lender will become liable for paying up on additional calls. Such calls will also be made when the company goes into liquidation, when the shares are not likely to be worth anything. Therefore partly paid shares are not recommended as security for lenders.

To sum up, quoted stocks and shares are easy to charge, easy to value and easy to realise, but there is a possibility of dilution or even disappearance of value over time.

8.4 Guarantees

> A **guarantee** is a promise or assurance offered by a third party to repay the lender if the borrower fails to repay the loan.

Guarantees are widely used by lenders. A guarantee must normally be in writing and must be signed by or on behalf of the party acting as the guarantor (Statute of Frauds 1677, s 4). The guarantee does not need to be notarised or registered. Due to developments in case law, the **guarantor** is required to sign a document indicating that the legal significance of making a guarantee has been fully understood. While the guarantor has a right to know the extent of liability, the lender needs to take care that the duty of confidentiality to the borrower is not breached.

8.4.1 Third-party security

Security provided by someone other than a borrower is known as 'third-party security'. A guarantee is probably the most common form of third-party security and is often unsupported (ie without any tangible security held in support).

Third-party security can take two forms:

1. a guarantee supported by a direct charge over an asset, given by the guarantor in support of their own guarantee;

2. a third-party form of charge directly in favour of the borrower rather than in support of the guarantee. This form gives the lender security for both the guarantee and for any liability in the name of the guarantor.

8.4.2 Nature and types

When the lender receives notice of the guarantor's death, mental incapacity or insolvency, it will be advisable to close any running account and route future transactions through a new account in order to avoid the rule in *Clayton's Case* from becoming operative. In *Bradford Old Bank Ltd v Sutcliffe* [1918], the liability of a mentally incapacitated guarantor was deemed to be satisfied by subsequent credits, because the account had not been closed when the guarantor became mentally incapable. However, providing the bank includes a clause in its guarantee form to expressly preclude the operation of *Clayton's Case* when failure to break an account upon determination of the guarantee will not adversely affect the bank (*Westminster Bank v Cond* [1940].

The guarantor who pays up on the borrower's default has the **right of subrogation** into the shoes of the lender and can assume the creditor's rights against the borrower who has defaulted. Many guarantees normally contain a clause that prevents the guarantor from standing in competition with the lender for the borrower's assets. In *Moschi v LEP Air Services Ltd* [1973] it was held that the guarantor's liability arose only when the principal debtor defaulted.

Guarantees will therefore have to contain an indemnity clause that secures the liability of the guarantor even if the borrower escapes liability. The lender will generally incorporate suitable clauses in the guarantee document to ensure that it has **simultaneous recourse** against both the borrower and the guarantor and can seek repayment from both or either to satisfy a debt. The lender can pursue the guarantor independently and is not bound to take action against the principal debtor first.

A guarantee will usually be **limited** to a specified amount and an assessment of the guarantor carried out to confirm the current, as well as future estimated, worth of the guarantor for the amount guaranteed. The practice of obtaining **unlimited** guarantee documents has been discouraged by the provisions of the Banking Code.

A bank guarantee is a **continuing guarantee** that covers a specific transaction. The amount of debt that is to be guaranteed and the duration of the guarantee are specified at the outset. A **continuing guarantee** lasts for an indefinite period and covers a flow of transactions within a specified overall limit.

Guarantees can be **joint** or **several**, or **joint and several**. Guarantees are generally drawn up as joint and several. Each co-guarantor is liable for the whole of the sum guaranteed.If a lender proceeds initially against only one or some of the guarantors, the remaining guarantors will continue to be liable and can be sued at a subsequent date (under the Civil Liberty (Contribution) Act 1978). A lender needs to ensure that any loan is released only after all of the guarantors have signed the guarantee document. If a co-guarantor fails or refuses to sign a guarantee, prior signatories to the guarantee can escape liability on the grounds that they signed on the understanding that all signatures would be obtained (*National Provincial Bank of England v Brackenbury* [1906]).

Guarantees can be given for loans by different types of entity, such as:

♦ individuals, eg a parent for a child (the child may be too young or have inadequate assets), or a child for a parent (the parent may be too old or have inadequate assets), or a wife for a husband, or a husband for a wife, etc;

♦ a solicitor for a client;

♦ a director for a company;

♦ a parent company for a subsidiary or related company;

♦ a government or central bank for a state-owned borrower.

After the abolition of the ultra vires rule, the capacity of a limited company to give a guarantee is clearly accepted. A guarantee given by a company will be shown as an off-balance-sheet contingent liability, unless the liability is crystallised by the invocation of the guarantee.

The Infants Relief Act 1874 invalidated certain contracts made by minors and prohibited actions to enforce contracts ratified after majority. Therefore loan contracts with minors were under most circumstances deemed to be void. In *Coutts v Browne-Lecky* [1947] a guarantee by an adult of a minor's overdraft was held to be void as the principal debt was void. In *R v Wilson* [1879] a minor was acquitted of leaving the country with the intention of defrauding creditors on the ground that, because the claim of the creditors rested on contracts declared 'absolutely void', the minor had, in fact, no creditors. After the Minors' Contracts Act 1987, however, the Infants Relief Act 1874 no longer invalidates certain contracts entered into by minors.

8.4.3 The advantages of guarantees as security

♦ Guarantees offered by high net worth entities can be valuable. Guarantees will be written to cover the value of the debt plus any accumulated interest and charges.

♦ In case of bankruptcy of the borrower, the trustee in bankruptcy has no claim on third-party security.

♦ Valuation is comparatively straightforward. The lender regularly obtains status reports on the guarantor.

♦ A guarantor has a strong incentive to ensure that the borrower remains creditworthy and capable of repaying the loan, particularly when the guarantor has provided security to back the guarantee.

♦ A guarantee is simple to take, involving just the obtention of signatures on a document and ensuring that the guarantor has the power of authority to execure the guarantee.

8.4.4 The disadvantages of guarantees as security

◆ Unlike borrowers who expect that a loan will have to be repaid, guarantors do not expect to actually be in a position in which they are asked to pay for the debts of the borrower. While a borrower uses the loan to acquire assets and increase the potential to generate cash, the guarantor might need to sell assets as well as reduce their own cash balances to meet the obligations under a guarantee. They are therefore likely to resist vigorously any claim made by a lender.

◆ The guarantor's own finances may not be adequate to absorb the shock of having to repay a borrower's debt. Deterioration in the guarantor's financial position might invalidate the assumptions made at the time of assessment of the guarantor's worth. A guarantor may not be subject to the same rigorous monitoring process as a borrower and the guarantor's financial position could have deteriorated, even to the point of insolvency, without the lender's knowledge.

◆ The guarantor might be a valued customer which the lender does not wish to alienate. In such circumstances, the lender might be reluctant to invoke the guarantee and lose the business provided by the guarantor.

◆ It is a general requirement that there should be sufficient legal 'consideration' for a guarantee. A guarantee must be backed by consideration unless it is executed as a deed or under seal. While certain situations, such as parental guarantee for a child's debt do not require consideration to be proved, the lack of consideration in certain other situations might invalidate a guarantee. If the consideration is further advances within an existing overdrawn account, the lender must prove that further advances were made (*Provincial Bank of Ireland v Donnell* [1934] and *Bank of Montreal v Sperling Hotel Co Ltd* [1973]).

◆ A guarantee may be negated on technicalities for not having been executed properly. Certain guarantees may be invalid from the outset. For example, a company is not able to guarantee a loan made to a director of that company.

◆ If a guarantor normally resides outside the country, the lending transaction might become subject to the jurisdiction of different laws.

◆ A borrower located in a different country might be able and willing to repay a debt, but prevented from repatriating the required funds by the central bank in that country. In such cases, a guarantor located outside the borrower's country may resist demands for payment with the argument that 'local payment' has been made by the borrower.

◆ The guarantor may be discharged if there is a change in the constitution or legal position of the parties. For example, the partner in a borrowing partnership firm may die, or a borrowing company may merge to form a new company (*Bradford Old Bank v Sutcliffe* [1883]).

◆ Legal objections can prevent a lender from realising a guarantee. In certain situations in which the guarantor has signed a guarantee without fully understanding the consequences, the courts have held that the guarantor is not liable for any debt.

◆ A number of guarantors have pleaded that they signed the guarantee under 'undue influence' and have successfully escaped liability. For example, in *Lloyds Bank Ltd v Bundy* [1975], Bundy Senior gave a guarantee for £1,500 in favour of Lloyds Bank to secure the business account of Bundy Junior. The guarantee was supported by a mortgage over a domestic property. At a subsequent meeting of Bundy Senior, Junior and a bank official, the guarantee was increased to £11,000. The son was made bankrupt by the bank who called on the guarantee. The High Court set the guarantee (and the mortgage) aside as Mr Bundy Senior was deemed to have been unduly influenced to enter into a contract which benefited others.

To sum up, guarantees are relatively easy to measure and take, but more difficult to monitor and realise.

8.5 Debentures: fixed and floating charges

8.5.1 Nature and types

The usage of the term **debenture** varies in different contexts and jurisdictions.

> An **unsecured debenture** is not secured by liens or pledges on specific assets, while a **secured debenture** is backed by assets. Here, a debenture is defined as a security interest that creates fixed and floating charges over all of the property of the borrower.

A debenture secured by land and/or buildings is called a **mortgage debenture**. Debentures are used by governments and large companies to obtain funds.

A **fixed charge** identifies and secures existing specific assets, such as land, buildings and machinery.
A **floating charge** is a security interest over, typically (but not necessarily), all of the assets of a company, which 'floats' until crystallised (becomes fixed), such crystallisation being usually triggered by a default by the borrower under the terms of the underlying loan documentation.

A floating charge enables assets such as stock, debtors/receivables, and cash, which fluctuate over time, to be caught as security. Floating charges cannot be created by individual persons or ordinary partnerships. Charges created by limited companies must be registered with Companies House within 21 days of creation (Companies Act 1985, s 395).

Re Yorkshire Woolcombers Association [1903] is generally cited as providing the most authoritative definition of a floating charge:

◆ it is a charge over a class of assets present and future;

◆ that class will be changing from time to time;

◆ until the charge crystallises and attaches to the assets, the chargor may carry on using the assets in the ordinary course of business.

More recently, in *National Westminster bank plc v Spectrum Plus Ltd* [2005] a floating charge was described as: 'not finally appropriated as a security for the payment of the debt until the occurrence of some future event. In the meantime the chargor is left free to use the charged asset and to remove it from the security' (see section 9.5.2).

8.5.2 The advantages of floating charges as security

◆ A floating charge enables the lender to take control over assets that are otherwise difficult to charge. The charge can cover goods in the process of manufacture, as well as future purchases.

◆ The procedure for creating a floating charge is fairly straightforward.

◆ A floating charge enables the lender to have priority of claim over unsecured creditors in the event of an insolvency.

◆ Floating charges are extremely flexible. From the lender's perspective, the security will cover each and every asset of the chargor. From the borrower's perspective, there is complete freedom to deal with the assets and dispose of them in the ordinary course of business.

◆ If necessary, the lender is able to crystallise the charge, and then sell off the available assets. As seen in section 2.1.4, the Enterprise Act 2002 has enabled floating chargeholders to appoint an administrator simply by filing a Notice of Appointment at court, without a court application and hearing.

◆ The lender is also able to preserve the company as a going concern by appointing an administrator or administrative receiver to take over the management and control of the business with a view to discharging the debt out of income or selling off the entire business as a going concern. Holders of floating charges created before the Enterprise Act came into force on 15 September 2003 will be able to choose to appoint an administrative receiver or an administrator. The ability of lenders who hold pre-existing floating charges to appoint an administrative receiver has, however, been since restricted under the Enterprise Act 2002.

8.5.3 The disadvantages of floating charges as security

◆ The valuation of assets covered by a floating charge is notoriously difficult. The price of goods may fluctuate, making valuation difficult.

◆ A floating charge cannot normally be enforced until it has crystallised. Because full control over the assets continues with the borrower prior to any crystallisation, the assets may be irretrievably lost or may have fallen in value before realisation can take place.

◆ The costs of realisation will be high. The lender might require the co-operation of the borrower for effecting a sale and such co-operation may not be forthcoming.

◆ In the event of an insolvency, the lender's claim will rank behind holders of a fixed security such as a mortgage or fixed charge, and preferred creditors (which since the Enterprise Act 2002, comprise wages only).

◆ As regards security interests created before any crystallisation, a fixed charge has priority over an earlier floating charge. This holds good even if a subsequent fixes charge-holder had notice of an earlier floating charge.

◆ Even after crystallisation, if the company creates a fixed charge over the charged assets, the subsequent fixed charge over the charged assets will have priority if the chargee (ie the new fixed-charge holder) did not have notice of the crystallisation. Floating charges take effect in equity only and consequently are defeated by a bona fide purchaser for value without notice of the charge.

◆ Stock may be subject to retention of title or *Romalpa* clauses and to dispute over priority of contending claims.

To sum up, floating charges are relatively easy to take, but more difficult to measure, monitor and realise.

8.6 The realisation of security

> **Realisation** is the process whereby the assets taken as security for advances are sold in order to repay a debt that is in default.

8.6.1 The action to be taken

The action to be taken by a lender in respect of realising available security will vary depending on the following.

◆ **The nature of the charge**. For example, whether legal or equitable. Generally, if a lender holds a legal charge, security can be realised without the need of obtaining the consent of either the borrower or the courts, whereas in the case of an equitable charge, the courts will need to be approached to authorise any action related to realisation.

◆ **The nature of the security**: the attractiveness of various forms of security in relation to of ease of realisation has been considered earlier. For example, realising the proceeds of a life policy that has been legally assigned to a lender will simply involve the issue of a notice to the insurer to remit the proceeds of the policy in settlement of loan default. The realisation of land will take much more time and will involve a variety of processes, such as valuation, advertisement, viewings, auction, conveyancing, etc.

◆ **The circumstances of the case**. The lender also needs to recognise that each case will be different and that the circumstances of each case will need to be carefully considered before any decision is made to realise the security that has been charged to them.

◆ **the other legal remedies available**. The lender will need to ensure that all other remedies against the borrower have been exhausted, and that proper procedures and legal requirements such as reminders and notices of default, have been served. Some of the issues relating to recovery action are discussed further in section 9.4.

8.6.2 Factors to be considered

The lender will need to consider carefully the various options available prior to the decision to realise the security. The factors or issues that will have to be borne in mind will include the following.

◆ The possibility of 'nursing' the borrower back to health so as to generate the revenues required to repay the debt.

◆ The possibility of selling the entire business as a going concern rather than sell the break-up assets, which will be worth much less.

◆ The position of the lender vis-à-vis other creditors in the order of priority in the event of any insolvency.

◆ The costs of realisation – whether the realisation proceeds will be adequate to cover the costs plus at least a part of the debt due.

◆ The likelihood of being able successfully to realise the security, which may depend upon legal and other factors. An unsuccessful legal action, for example, will result in additional costs being incurred during the attempt to realise security without any attendant benefits.

◆ The various risks of realisation need to be evaluated carefully.

While security serves to mitigate credit risk, it carries its own risks (Bessis, 2002).

Figure 8.1   Realisation risk

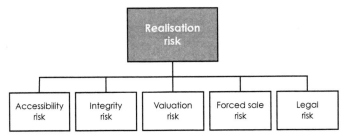

◆ **Accessibility risk** is the risk that the assets secured to the lender may not be readily accessible to enable them to be seized and sold.

◆ **Integrity risk** is the risk that the assets seized by the lender with a view to their sale are damaged or have become defective. Assets can be damaged either inadvertently or deliberately, prior to or in the process of being seized.

◆ **Valuation risk** is the risk that the value of the assets is not readily ascertainable. Valuation will be dependent upon the existence of an active secondary market, the volatility in the market and market demand.

◆ **Forced sale risk** is the risk of loss of asset value due to the sale of assets under the constraints imposed by the lender or by law.

◆ **Legal risk** can arise due to disputes in law in a number of ways.

   – Borrowers have successfully avoided giving up security by arguing that **undue influence** was exerted on the borrower or guarantor. As seen earlier, undue influence has been proved in certain circumstances to exist in cases of unequal bargaining power, eg between a husband and his wife (*National Westminster Bank plc v Morgan* [1985], *Barclays Bank v O'Brien* [1994], *Royal Bank of Scotland plc v Etridge* [2001], and between an elderly parent and adult child (*Bullock v Lloyds Bank Ltd* [1955] and *Avon Finance Co Ltd v Bridger* [1985]).

- The lender can by found guilty of **misrepresentation** if the lender had been in possession of facts that should have given rise to a suspicion that the principal debtor was defrauding the guarantor and if these were withheld from the guarantor (*National Provincial Bank of England v Glanusk* [1913].

- The defence of signing a document by **mistake**, ie *non est factum* (not my act), is available to those who were unable to understand the purpose of the document that was signed, or those who signed a document that was not the document that was intended to be signed (*Foster v McKinnon* [1869] and *Sanders v Anglia Building Society* [1971]).

The Enterprise Act 2002 is said to have encouraged a number of borrowers to avoid their debt obligations by resorting to insolvency. When a borrower goes into **insolvency**, any assets realised by the lender prior to insolvency might be subject to the risk of being considered as a preference and/or a transaction at undervalue.

- **Preference**: if a person or company transfers assets or pays a debt to a creditor shortly before going into insolvency, that payment or transfer can be set aside on the application of the trustee in bankruptcy or liquidator as a preference. For a transaction to be deemed to be a preference, it should be demonstrated that:

    - the person or company was insolvent at the time the payment was made;

    - the person or company went into insolvency within a specified 'relevant time' after making the payment;

    - the payment had the effect of putting the creditor in a better position than other unsecured creditors.

When a transaction is declared to be a preference, arrangements will be made for restoring the position to that which it would have been had that preference not been made. Sections 239 and 340 of the Insolvency Act 1986 describe the circumstances under which an unfair preference may be deemed to have been given by an insolvent company and individual respectively.

- **Undervalue**: a transaction entered into by an individual or company which subsequently goes into insolvency can be deemed to be a transaction at an undervalue, which the court can order to be set aside, provided that the following conditions are met:

    - the consideration received in the transaction, 'in money or money's worth', is significantly less than the value provided;

    - the transaction was entered into during the 'relevant time' immediately prior to the bankruptcy; and

    - at the time of the transaction, the borrower was unable to pay the debts as they fell due, or became unable to pay its debts as they fell due as a result of the transaction.

Following *Standard Chartered Bank v Walker* [1982], lenders ensure that professional agents are appointed to ensure that any sale can be seen to be at market valuation (or near to).

In such circumstances, the court will arrange to restore the position to that which it would have been had the transaction not been entered into. Sections

238 and 339 of the Insolvency Act 1986 describe the circumstances under which a transaction by an insolvent company and individual, respectively, may be deemed to be at an undervalue.

The 'relevant time' for preferential or undervalue transactions is laid down in ss 240 and 341 respectively for a company and a person. In the case of a person, for example, for a preference that is not a transaction of undervalue, the 'relevant time' is two years if the beneficiary is an associate, and six months in other cases.

Realisation of security is often costly, time-consuming and inefficient (Willingham, 1997). The realisation of security will involve the break-up or forced sale of the assets. The value of such assets will be less under such circumstances than if the borrower had been sold as a going concern. Therefore realisation of security should be a last resort when all other viable alternatives have failed.

There is a tendency among many lenders readily to grant credit facilities to prospective borrowers on the strength of the security available without paying adequate attention to the viability of the loan proposal. It is important that lenders realise the dangers in this approach. Security is obtained only as a backup, and more as an incentive for the borrower's personal covenant to repay (ie the borrower can be sued notwithstanding the provision of security). It should always be remembered that the primary security is the borrower and that the borrower's activities need to generate the resources required for repayment of borrowings. This will be the primary source of repayment, rather than any security. It will be unwise to assume that the costs of default will be entirely compensated by obtaining security (Chant, 1970). Lenders are rarely able to recover both loan and costs by the realisation of security.

Conclusion

Security can take the form of proprietary security, possessory security, intangible security, financial instruments such as shares and bonds, insurance policies, guarantees with or without security owned by the third party, choses in action, and debentures that might include both fixed and floating charges.

The lender therefore needs to be aware of the various forms of security and their relative advantages and disadvantages.

While security serves to mitigate credit risk, it carries its own risks. Collateral risk or realisation risk refers to the combination of risks faced by a lender who needs to realise the security obtained towards repayment of debt. These risks include accessibility risk, integrity risk, forced sale risk and legal risks that might involve undue influence, misrepresentation and mistake of fact. Further, when a borrower goes into insolvency, any assets realised by the lender prior to insolvency might be subject to the risk of being considered as a preference and/or a transaction at undervalue. Therefore realisation of security should only be resorted when all other viable alternatives have failed.

Further reading

Dennant, A. (2006) 'Security – a basic review' *ifs* Lead tutor article.

Topic 8

Review questions, activities and case study

The following review questions, activities and case study are designed to increase your understanding of the material you have just studied.

◆ The **review questions** are designed so that you can check your understanding of this topic.

◆ Completion of the **activities** will give you further opportunity to research and understand, in more depth, the themes running through this topic.

◆ The **case study** encourages you to think further about the application of the content of this topic.

The answers to the questions and case study are provided at the end of these learning materials. Please note that the activities are open-ended and therefore suitable 'answers' may not be provided.

Review questions

1. Distinguish between 'proprietary security' and 'possessory security'.

2. What are the advantages and disadvantages of taking the following forms of security?

   ◆ Land and property.

   ◆ Life insurance policies.

   ◆ Stocks and shares.

   ◆ Guarantees.

3. Examine the nature of a floating charge. What are its advantages and disadvantages?

4. Examine the various components of realisation risk.

5. What are the implications of transactions at undervalue and preference for a lender in connection with the realisation of security?

Activity

Activity 1

> Where should a mortgagee register its interest after taking a charge over (1) Registered Land (2) Unregistered land?

Activity 2

> When taking a subsequent mortgage, what action – in addition to registering the charge as in A above 0 – should the mortgagee take?

Activity 3

> Ensure that you understand the full range of policies available through your own organisation or its subsidiaries.Differentiate between endowment policies, whole life policies, pension plans, Life protection insurance and which are suitable to be taken as security by the lender.

Activity 4

> Guarantors are protected by common law. Most of their rights are removed by clauses in the bank's guarantee form. Examine your own bank's form

and note how it deals with many of the disadvantages mentioned in section 8.4.4.

Activity 5

Visit http://www.publications.parliament.uk/pa/ld199899/ldjudgmt/jd991021/barc.htm and read the case of *Barclays Bank plc v Boulter and Boulter* [1999] decided by the House of Lords. Examine some of the issues raised about undue influence, misrepresentation and third party guarantees.

Case study – *Barclays Bank plc v O'Brien* [1994]

Mr Nicholas Edward O'Brien and Mrs Bridget Mary O'Brien were husband and wife. The matrimonial home situated at Farnham Lane in Slough was in their joint names. Mr O'Brien was a chartered accountant and had an interest in a company called Heathrow Fabrications Ltd, which had an account with the Woolwich branch of Barclays Bank. In the first three months of 1987, the company frequently exceeded its overdraft facility of £40,000. Mr O'Brien told Mr Tucker the manager of the Woolwich branch, that he was remortgaging the matrimonial home. The overdraft limit was raised at that stage to £60,000 for one month. Even though no additional security was provided, by 15 June 1987, the company's overdraft had risen to £98,000 and its cheques were being dishonoured.

On 22 June 1987, Mr O'Brien and Mr Tucker agreed: (1) that the company's overdraft limit would be raised to £135,000 reducing to £120,000 after three weeks; (2) that Mr O'Brien would guarantee the company's indebtedness; and (3) that Mr O'Brien's liability would be secured by a second charge on the matrimonial home.

The necessary security documents were prepared by the bank. They consisted of an unlimited guarantee by Mr O'Brien of the company's liability and a legal charge by both Mr and Mrs O'Brien of the matrimonial home to secure any liability of Mr O'Brien to the bank. Mr Tucker arranged for the documents, together with a side letter, to be sent to the Burnham branch of the bank for execution by Mr and Mrs O'Brien. In a covering memorandum, Mr Tucker requested the Burnham branch to advise the O'Briens as to the current level of the facilities amounting to £107,000 and the projected increase to £135,000. The Burnham branch was also asked to ensure that the O'Briens were 'fully aware of the nature of the documentation to be signed and advised that if they are in any doubt they should contact their solicitors before signing.'

The Burnham branch, however, did not give Mrs O'Brien any explanation of the effect of the documents. No one suggested that she should take independent legal advice. She did not read the documents or the side letter. In July 1987, she signed the legal charge and side letter, and her signature was witnessed by the bank clerk. She was not given a copy of the guarantee.

Heathrow Fabrications Ltd struggled to survive and, by October 1987, its indebtedness to the bank was over £154,000. In November 1987, demand was made on Mr O'Brien under his guarantee. When the demand was not met, possession proceedings under the legal charge were brought by the bank against Mr and Mrs O'Brien. Mrs O'Brien defended these proceedings by alleging that she was induced to execute the legal charge on the matrimonial home by the undue influence of Mr O'Brien and by his misrepresentation that the charge was to secure only £60,000 and that even this liability would be released in a short time when the house was remortgaged.

The House of Lords found that 'the tenderness of the law towards married women is due to the fact that, even today, many wives repose confidence and trust in their husbands in relation to their financial affairs. The 'tenderness' shown by the law to married women is not based on the marriage ceremony but reflects the underlying risk of one cohabitee exploiting the emotional involvement and trust of the other'.

But the House of Lords also found that 'if the doctrine of notice is properly applied, there is no need for the introduction of a special equity in these types of cases'. In the case of husband and wife living together, constructive notice would be presumed from the fact that the transaction was, on its face, not to the financial advantage of the wife. The bank should have been put on inquiry as to the circumstances in which Mrs O'Brien had agreed to stand as surety for the debt of her husband. Mrs O'Brien had signed the documents without any warning of the risks or any recommendation to take legal advice. The bank had constructive notice of the wrongful misrepresentation made by Mr O'Brien to Mrs O'Brien, but had failed to take 'reasonable steps'. Failure on the part of the lender to take these reasonable steps resulted in the obligations undertaken by Mrs O'Brien being set aside.

Following a similar case – *Royal Bank of Scotland v Etridge* [2001] – guidelines have been produced for solicitors acting in cases where one party to a 'non-commercial' relationship – usually, but not exclusively, a wife – is standing as guarantor of the other party's business debts, and banks are required to follow even more rigorous procedures to ensure that issues relating to undue influence are avoided.

1 What was the security obtained by Barclays Bank for the business loan given to Mr O'Brien's company?

2 What was the misrepresentation made by Mr O'Brien to Mrs O'Brien?

3 Was the lender's legal charge on the property set aside because of the 'tenderness of the law' towards wives?

4 How did the lender fail to take 'reasonable steps'?

5 What are the lessons here for lenders?

Topic 9

The lending cycle – the monitoring and control process

Learning outcomes

By the end of this topic, students should be able to understand the life cycle of a lending facility after the credit-granting process has been completed, loan monitoring and control procedures, and the actions that the lender may decide to take when the customer's ability to repay is under threat.

Learning areas include:

◆ monitoring and control, including information sources for review;

◆ early warning signals;

◆ recovery action;

◆ insolvency options.

9.1 The need for monitoring and control

Lending is an activity that carries risk, but appropriate follow up action can minimise credit losses. Monitoring and control of lending activities are essential, particularly because banks are subject to the problem of moral hazard (Carletti et al, 2007).

Moral hazard is the risk that the borrower will act in an imprudent or reckless manner because the lender might have more to lose than the borrower.

Credit facilities need to be monitored in order to:

◆ be fully aware of the up-to-date situation to ensure that the borrower is creditworthy and that borrowing remains within the capacity to repay;

◆ detect adverse trends and potential problem loans as early as possible;

◆ ensure that documentation and charges over collateral security remain up to date;

◆ ensure that legal and regulatory requirements are met;

◆ confirm information provided by the customer about income and outgoings;

◆ assess the overall condition and continued profitability of the loan portfolio;

- ◆ set aside provisions for loan losses;
- ◆ enforce an appropriate credit environment within the lending organisation.

9.2   Information sources for review

Research has found that lenders' investments in both branch network density and human capital (personnel) contribute to their monitoring ability; increased information flows enable lenders to monitor borrower activity and cash flows, thereby decreasing the amount of credit losses (Hyytinen and Toivanen, 2004). Sources of information are both internal and external, and the information can be both hard and soft, as seen in section 6.2.2.

Figure 9.1   Sources of information for monitoring and control

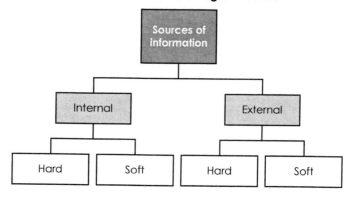

9.2.1 Internal sources

Internal sources of **hard information** include:

- ◆ computer printouts furnishing borrower account information, such as balance trends;
- ◆ borrower account statements, showing turnover, transactions and any extraordinary items;
- ◆ debit and credit vouchers, showing details of any specific transactions;
- ◆ customer databases.

Internal sources of **soft information** could be:

- ◆ staff who interact with the borrower as part of:
  - – head office,
  - – branch offices,
  - – the marketing department,

- – the customer services department,
- – other deparments;
◆ personal interviews with the borrower.

9.2.2 External sources

External sources of **hard information** could include those available from the borrower, such as:

◆ audited financial statements and accounts;

◆ management accounts;

◆ sales forecasts;

◆ the stock position;

◆ a list of pending advance orders;

◆ copies of quarterly tax returns;

◆ VAT, income tax and corporate tax returns;

◆ information about companies with similar businesses.

External sources other than the borrower could be:

◆ governmental, such as the Department for Business, Enterprise and Regulatory Reform (BERR), the Office for National Statistics and other departments;

◆ non-government organisations (NGOs) such as the British Chambers of Commerce (BCC) and Finance and Leasing Association (FLA);

◆ commercial and semi-official sources, such as Dun & Bradstreet directories and Mintel;

◆ international organisations, such as the World Trade Organisation (WTO) trade associations;

◆ newspapers and journals, such as the *Financial Times* and *The Economist*;

◆ libraries;

◆ the Internet.

External sources of **soft information** could include:

◆ telephone conversations and meetings at the borrower's premises with the management and staff employed by the borrower belonging to various departments of the business;

◆ trade associations, such as the British Bankers' Association (BBA), the Association of British Insurers (ABI) and the Finance and Leasing Association (FLA).

Networking events, meetings and personal interaction generate soft information that is difficult to quantify but often even more useful than hard information.

9.3   The detection of problems

9.3.1   Early warning signals

Early warning signs for personal customers are fairly straightforward. If the borrowing is a loan, then the monthly repayment may be missed, or may cause a current account to become out of order. If borrowing is by way of overdraft, then a normal activity cycle would see monthly salary repaying old borrowing, with the account becoming increasingly overdrawn until receipt of the following salary. Excesses will be flagged by way of a daily out of order report. In addition, there is a risk that while an account may remain within its borrowing limits, an increasing 'hardcore' element of borrowing may not be cleared each month. This may lead to a need to take action to control the situation at some point.

For business customers, some early warning signals are as follows.

◆ A delay in the auditing/submission of financial statements, which could indicate a reluctance of the borrower to submit unfavourable financial results to the lender.

◆ A deterioration in financial ratios and worrying trends in financial statements.

◆ Cash flow problems, declining cash balances and large increases in receivables, short-term debt, inventory and fixed assets.

◆ Deteriorating relations with trade suppliers.

◆ A decrease in inventory turnover, or a decrease in receivables turnover.

◆ Delays or an increase in accounts payable and short-term creditors not being repaid by the end of the seasonal cycle.

◆ A decline in sales or unanticipated changes in demand due to obsolescence.

◆ Reduced credits to the account or persistent overdrawings.

◆ Loss of key customers.

◆ Lockouts, strikes or a general deterioration of labour relations.

◆ Production and delivery problems, negative press reports.

◆ Adverse environmental factors or natural disasters.

◆ Delayed payments of principal and interest.

◆ A decline in margin and an increase in loan to value (LTV).

◆ Loan proceeds being used for unintended purposes.

◆ Frequent turnover in management and personnel.

◆ The expiry or cancellation of insurance policies.

◆ Second charges on security filed against the borrower by other creditors.

◆ Notice of legal action against the borrower.

◆ Notice of a tax liens or garnishee order against the borrower.

- Deterioration in the rapport with the borrower, unexplained changes in the borrower's attitude or the reluctance of borrower to communicate.

- The death or departure of key persons.

- Health, marital or personal problems.

- Overcapitalisation and an inability to use available resources profitably.

- Growing too quickly or overtrading.

> **Overcapitalisation** is a situation in which the capital used by a business is excessive for its needs. It is characterised by excessive stocks, debtors and cash, leading to a low return on investment, and long-term funds tied up in non-earning short-term assets.

Symptoms that might enable a lender to identify overcapitalisation are:

- liquidity too high – increasing current ratio and quick ratio;

- gearing too low – lower gearing ratio;

- too low a turnover to justify the investment in assets, resulting in idle cash and takeover threats;

- a drop in the ratio of sales to equity;

- a high ratio of fixed assets to working capital, which could indicate overinvestment in assets in anticipation of sales that did not materialise;

- inefficient working capital management;

- excessive cash generation in relation to the availability of investment opportunities.

> **Overtrading** is a situation in which a business attempts to take on too large a volume of activities in relation to available levels of working capital. It is characterised by a volume of business activity that is excessive in relation to finance provided by owners or shareholders and an undue reliance on external finance. It means that the business is attempting too much too quickly.

Symptoms that might enable a lender to identify overtrading are:

- liquidity too low – declining current ratio and quick ratio;

- net working capital tends to decline and may even become negative;

- a decline in the ratio of debtors to creditors, with creditors being asked to wait longer;

- gearing too high – higher gearing ratio;

- too high a turnover in relation to investment, resulting in cash shortages and liquidity crises;

- sharp increases in the ratio of sales to equity;

- a severe shortage of cash.

Undercapitalisation is considered by both owners and official receivers to be the leading cause of insolvency (Hall and Young, 1991).

It is also important that there is in place a system of incentives that rewards careful lending. The best early warning system will not work if nobody wants to look or listen, a situation that has arisen when incentive schemes are skewed in favour of loan quantity rather than loan quality.

9.3.2 Reasons for losses

Losses can arise when lending principles are not appropriately and adequately recognised or incorporated in lending polices. Accordingly, it will be worth revisiting the lending principles listed in section 1.5, because failure to observe these principles can lead to losses.

Some reasons for losses include the following:

◆ excessively lax covenants – increased competition for customers may lead to an easing of credit standards to obtain new business;

◆ encouraging borrowers to borrow more than they need, or to falsify information on the application information, or to self-certify application details;

◆ lending to those who are clearly unable to afford the repayments;

◆ economic recession and business failure;

◆ excessively rigid covenants with which the borrower is unable to comply;

◆ a failure to arrange for the valuation of security;

◆ the overvaluation of security;

◆ lending against fictitious security;

◆ inadequate margins or excessive loan to value (LTV);

◆ a failure to complete documentation;

◆ the release of the loan prior to the completion of documentation;

◆ renewing a loan for increasing amounts, with no additional security taken;

◆ repeatedly renewing a loan in order to cover unpaid interest;

◆ a failure to analyse a borrower's cash flows;

◆ a failure to review the condition of a lending frequently enough;

◆ loan officers having too close a relationship with the borrower;

◆ loan officers having too distant a relationship with the borrower;

◆ loan officers exceeding their discretionary powers or limits;

◆ loan officers being too aggressive and dominating;

◆ lending in areas where the lender lacks expertise;

- loan diversion to the borrower's personal use and not applied for the purpose for which it was granted;

- no attempt being made to verify the purpose for which the loan was applied;

- the repayment plan not being clearly set out;

- a failure to ensure the regular receipt of borrower's financial statements;

- a failure to follow established procedures;

- ignoring frequent overdrawings without investigating the reasons;

- loans to a new business with inexperienced management;

- a failure to get credit reports;

- a failure to take note of negative credit reports;

- poor communication with the borrower;

- a failure to inspect the borrower's business premises;

- a failure to take quick recovery action when deterioration becomes obvious;

- a failure to note early warning signals.

9.3.3 Control measures

We have seen the various means by which lending can be monitored to ensure the continuing safety, liquidity and profitability of advances. Should these signs indicate that an advance is at risk, we must invoke the final stage in the lending cycle, that of control.

Where an advance is by way of loan, then failure to receive a repayment from another financial services provider should give cause for contact with the customer to elicit the reason for this lapse, with subsequent action for recovery dependent on the response which ensues.

Where by overdraft, it may become necessary to return items such as cheques or regular payments to restrict borrowing to within agreed limits.

If a regular payment is in respect of a loan instalment, then this payment should not be made. Making the payment will simply keep the loan in order at expense of the overdraft. As the loan will certainly have a formal loan agreement which will provide a structure for recovery in the event of default (or may indeed be secured) it is better for the lender to not make the payment.

If the payment is in respect of an insurance premium which relates to items charged as security, (either a monthly premium on a life assurance policy or on fire insurance relating to property which you have charged) then these payments should be made to ensure the integrity of your charge.

9.3.3.1 Returning cheques

Although unpleasant, it is often necessary to return items to control the spending of those who cannot control their own. If we do not, then we will end up with a doubtful debt and eventually a bad debt. These are both failures for lenders as they represent lost money (which was not the lender's in the first place) and lost profit, which reduces the returns for investors in the lender.

Before returning a cheque or standing order, the following questions should be considered.

◆ Has the customer contacted you advising you of the breach, making an agreement to restore the out of order position?

◆ What damage will 'bouncing' do to the customers' credit worthiness and reputation in the world at large?

◆ What is the debit for? If it relates to your loan security, eg life or building insurance, then you may wish to pay the debit.

◆ Does the customer have credit balances on other accounts that can be set off? For example, if a customer has £10,000 in a deposit it would be foolhardy to bounce a cheque for £150.

◆ Is the customer the managing director of your largest customer, or a partner in a major professional firm that banks with you?

◆ Can the customer be contacted? Never return an item without making every effort to speak to the customer. Obviously, take care here. If the account concerned is a sole account don't tell a partner (even if they have a joint account) of the position. When contacting a customer at work be very discrete. Don't leave a message with a receptionist asking Fred to phone you about his overdraft!

The advantage of contacting the customer is two fold. The customer may be aware of the breach and is arranging for funds to be paid in to correct. The breach may be a simple oversight and the customer will again organise funds to be paid in later in the day.

The second benefit is that, if the customer has no explanation for the excess and offers no plans to regularise the situation, then you can tell the customer that you will be returning the item. This leaves the customer in no doubt as to your proposed action and will often change their position. Even if it does not, then at least the customer has chance to warn the payee and attempt to limit the damage.

If the customer cannot be contacted, you will need to inspect the branch records. Have items been returned before? If not, it would strongly suggest that you consult with a colleague before making the decision to return.

Although returning the cheque will regularise the account, it may also have a number of other consequences. Firstly, the hitherto elusive customer may suddenly appear. Secondly, the action will have stated your intent to control the account. Thirdly, you may lose the account – and any associated accounts.

9.4 The stages of recovery

9.4.1 Recovery action

A good advance will be repaid with interest on the due date – but a lender will need to take recovery action in respect of advances that are not repaid promptly. **Recovery action** would need to include the realisation of any security that might have been provided by the borrower. As indicated in section 9.4, there will be a number of stages in the recovery action. Firstly, the loan will have to be recalled or called up if it is not already in default due to non-observance of loan covenants. The lender might need to negotiate with the borrower about any debt moratorium or debt restructuring. Then the lender will have to decide if the loan amount warrants legal action and attendant costs. In the case of smaller amounts, the lender may find it more cost-effective simply to write off the loan amount after notifying the credit rating agencies of the default. In the case of larger amounts, the creditor would want to initiate legal proceedings for the recovery of sums due. Such legal proceedings might, in the ultimate analysis, involve the insolvency of the debtor.

Sometimes, lenders may wish to effect a **rescue** rather than a closure. Nursing a sick company back to health can be more beneficial than closing it. 'Company doctors' have been brought in as part of the process of establishing a rescue culture, because 'a saved company is a continuing customer ...Businesses have their own networks, and banks that develop a reputation for rescuing only their own position rather than the total business will, over time, suffer'. (Touhey, 1997)

For lenders, receivership should be the last option. Irrecoverable debt can also be converted into equity or some form of convertible loan stock, thereby addressing weaknesses in capital structure.

9.5   Insolvency

Insolvency is defined as a condition that arises when a borrower is unable to pay debts when they fall due for repayment.

In pursuing insolvency, the lender would need to prove that the borrower is unable to pay, or has no reasonable prospect of paying, the debts. Once the lender has sent a petition to the court, a hearing takes place and an order is made if the court feels that this is the appropriate outcome.

For an individual, the court will appoint a Trustee in Bankruptcy, often the Official Receiver. The Official Receiver will make an application to the court claiming assets and any income that exceeds the amount needed by the bankrupt to cover essential living costs for self and family.

For a limited company, a meeting of creditors will appoint either an administrator or an administrative receiver as applicable. **Liquidation** is terminal for a company. It ceases to trade and the liquidator is left to dispose of the assets. The liquidator's objective is to maximise realisation from the sale of assets, collection of debts etc, in order to pay a dividend to creditors, if at all possible. Directors are not liable for the debts of the company unless they have signed personal guarantees to that effect. The liquidator will also review the company's affairs with a view to reporting on the conduct of the directors. Any offences highlighted in the report may lead to directors being disqualified from acting in that capacity in the future.

9.5.1   Insolvency options

It may be in the interests of creditors that the business is allowed to continue trading as it may be possible for the business to trade out of its present difficulties. There are various options available to creditors should they wish to pursue this line.

◆ **Company voluntary arrangement (CVA)**: this is a contract between a company and its creditors, which offers the creditors a better financial outcome than would be achieved in a liquidation. The company may continue to trade, usually under the control of its directors, with a view to paying creditors either out of future profits, or from a more beneficial realisation of the company's assets, or both. The appointed insolvency practitioner, known as the supervisor, monitors the company's performance to ensure the terms of the proposal are complied with.

Individuals are dealt with in a similar way and this is known as an **Individual voluntary arrangement (IVA)**. This is a formal arrangement that begins with a proposal to creditors to pay part or all of an individuals debts. Application is made to the court with the help of an insolvency practitioner (supervisor). Any agreement reached with creditors will be binding on them.

◆ **Administrative receivership**: an administrative receiver can only be appointed by a holder of a valid floating charge who acts to achieve the best possible outcome for the charge-holder. The administrative receiver only deals with assets covered by the security under which he or she is appointed. The administrative receiver may decide that the company should cease trading and its assets sold on a break-up basis; that the company should be sold as a going concern; that only part of the company should be sold, or that it should continue trading under supervision, etc. Changes in legislation (see Enterprise Act 2002) have introduced restrictions on the ability of holders of a floating charge to appoint an administrative receiver. The appointment of an administrator by a charge-holder is likely to become a more usual approach.

◆ **Administration order**: an administrator will have a duty to all the company's creditors, not just the floating charge-holder(s), irrespective of whoever appointed them. A business in trouble often seeks protection from creditor pressure and the new regime introduced in September 2003 makes it much simpler and quicker for a company to enter Administration, buying time to get its affairs in order and to decide the best way forward. An administrator can be appointed in or out of court by the directors, the holder of a floating charge or a creditor if they have concerns about the financial well-being of their customer.

◆ **Liquidation** is a formal procedure whereby a liquidator is appointed to 'wind up' the affairs of a company. There are two ways to liquidate a company.

   – Creditors' voluntary liquidation (CVL): the decision to commence liquidation is voluntarily made by the directors/shareholders of a company. The shareholders nominate an insolvency practitioner as liquidator subject to the agreement of creditors at a creditors' meeting.

   – Compulsory liquidation. This ensues when a creditor has successfully presented a winding-up petition to the court. The Official Receiver is appointed. Any available assets will need to be realised and distributed. The process is much slower and more expensive than a CVL.

9.5.2 Order of priority on liquidation

There are strict rules of priority as regards the order in which creditors are paid on the liquidation of a firm. Generally, the priority of claims on an **insolvent company's assets** will be determined in the following order.

1. Secured creditors. If a lender or other party holds a fixed and floating charge over the assets of the company (a **debenture**), then they will be entitled to realisations from 'fixed charge assets' first. For example, these might be freehold property, fixed plant and machinery and realisations from investments.

   Book debts used to fall under this category. It was established in cases such as *Siebe Gorman & Co Ltd v Barclays Bank Ltd* [1979] that it is possible to obtain a fixed charge on book debts. But the decision by the Privy Council in June 2001 in the case of *Brumark Investments Ltd* [2001] created uncertainty over whether a lender could have a valid fixed charge over book debts. This has been resolved by the House of Lords decision in *National Westminster Bank plc v Spectrum Plus Ltd* [2005]. The Lords found that, under the terms of the debenture, the bank required the customer to pay debts into the account with the bank, but left the customer free to collect the debts in the normal course of business and to draw on the account for normal business purposes. This freedom to draw on the proceeds meant that the charge over book debts could not be categorised as fixed. Thus it is no longer possible to have a fixed charge over book debts, which will now be subject to a floating charge only. Due to the Enterprise Act 2002, this is now only of historical significance.

2. Expenses of liquidation. Costs of the liquidation are met out of the company's remaining assets.

3. Claims of preferential creditor. After the abolition of the preferential status of the Crown creditors introduced by the Enterprise Act in September 2003 in the vast majority of cases, only employees for wages (up to £800 per person) and holiday pay rank ahead of the floating charge creditor.

4. Floating charge. For floating charges created after 15 September 2003, however, the holders will have to give up a percentage of realisations to unsecured, non-preferential creditors. This will be 50% of the first £10,000 and 20% thereafter, to a maximum asset value limit of £600,000.

5. Debts that are neither preferential nor postponed. If there is anything left, the unsecured creditors are paid out *pari passu* – that is, ranking equally – in accordance with their claims.

6. Interest on debts.

7. Claims of postponed creditors, for example, unauthorised investment business.

8. Surplus assets – these are distributed to the shareholders.

On 15 September 2003, the corporate provisions of the Enterprise Act 2002 came into effect, abolishing the rights of the Inland Revenue & HM Customs and Excise (now HM Revenue & Customs) to establish preferential claims; it now ranks with trade creditors for any dividends. This means that creditors as a whole are more likely to receive a dividend in insolvencies than was previously the case.

The priority of claims on an **insolvent individual's assets** will be determined in the following order.

1. Secured creditors.

2. Expenses of the bankruptcy.

3. Claims of preferential creditors.

4. Debts that are neither preferential nor postponed.

5. Interest on debt.

6. Debts to postponed creditors, eg money owed to the spouse of the bankrupt at the date of the bankruptcy order.

7. Surplus returned to the bankrupt.

Insolvency entails advantages as well as disadvantages.

9.5.3 Advantages of insolvency

◆ There is a possibility that some recovery will be possible by means of following a prescribed order of distribution of the bankrupt's assets.

◆ All creditors are dealt with equitably, as set out in the order of priority and as required by law.

◆ Creditors feel more comfortable when a trustee in bankruptcy or an insolvency practitioner is involved in the process.

◆ The process allows a full investigation of the borrower's affairs.

◆ Borrowers are likely to co-operate when it is perceived as providing peace of mind as against the anxiety of being continually indebted.

9.5.4 Disadvantages of insolvency

◆ If the lender has not secured a fixed charge against specific security, the chances of recovery recede.

◆ Insolvency proceedings involve additional costs, in the form of professional fees and the additional time involved in complying with statutory requirements.

◆ Borrowers are likely to resist when faced with the possibility of losing control over their assets, including their home, and also for various reasons including restrictions that might arise in relation to future credit, occupations and professions.

Conclusion

The credit granting process needs to be followed by the credit monitoring and credit recovery processes as appropriate. Monitoring and control of lending activities are essential, particularly because banks are subject to the problem of moral hazard. Sources of information for review are both internal and external, and the information can be both hard and soft. Detection of early warning signals is part of the credit monitoring process.

Monitoring and control is an essential part of the lending cycle. Among the reports and printouts, it is important not to lose sight of the human issues. There is no substitute for communication with our customers – a call or meeting will often produce the best results – both for them and for your bank. You would be wise, therefore, to make every effort to make personal contact – it might not work, but if it does, your efforts are often rewarded.

Alongside that, there is another important point to remember – a deteriorating account means the customer has a problem and we all, at some time or other, find our problems hard to talk about. They may feel uncomfortable, embarrassed, and ashamed. It would be unusual indeed for a customer to simply spill all their problems before you – this means you are part banker, part investigator, and part counsellor. You will need to probe, to ask indirect and open questions, and above all, show a little patience in getting the answers.

Insolvency is defined as a condition that arises when a borrower is unable to pay debts when they fall due for repayment. Insolvency options include administrative receivership, compulsory liquidation, creditors' voluntary liquidation (CVL) and administration orders for company voluntary arrangements (CVA) or informal arrangements.

Lenders need to provide for loan losses by debit to the profit and loss account. A portion of the profits are set aside in the form of provision for bad and doubtful debts. Any losses will have to be written off by debit to the provision for bad and doubtful debts account.

Further reading

Bessis, J. (2002) *Risk Management in Banking*, John Wiley and Sons Ltd, Chichester.

Topic 9

Review questions

The following review questions are designed to increase your understanding of the material you have just studied.

◆ The **review questions** are designed so that you can check your understanding of this topic.

The answers to the questions are provided at the end of these learning materials.

Review questions

?

1. Identify some of the reasons for monitoring accounts.

2. Identify some of the internal and external sources of information that might be available when conducting reviews.

3. What are the early warning signals of problem lending?

4. Examine some of the measures that might be adopted for controlling credit risk.

Topic 10
The impact of lending and social responsibility

Learning outcomes

By the end of this topic, students should be able to understand the impact of lending on the economy and society and to recognise the need for responsible lending.

Learning areas include:

◆ the economic and social effects of lending;

◆ corporate social responsibility (CSR);

◆ the importance of responsible lending.

10.1 The economic and social effects of lending

Lending has far-reaching consequences: 'Systematic evidence over the last decade has documented a robust and positive relationship between finance and economic development' (Chakraborty and Ray, 2006). Lending can generate powerful economic and social effects that can be both beneficial and detrimental to society as a whole.

Lending can lead to huge economic and social benefits:

◆ lending drives economic growth;

◆ lending leads to the more efficient allocation and utilisation of resources in the economy;

◆ lending stimulates higher levels of saving – a part of the income earned from lending is used to reward savers who provide some of the funds required by lenders;

◆ lending promotes liquidity and makes available funds for investment and consumption;

◆ lending improves the availability of funds to higher risk ventures;

◆ social lending makes funds available to disadvantaged sections of society at low cost.

Lending can also have detrimental effects on the economy:

◆ irresponsible lending encourages irresponsible borrowing. For example, there have been instances of borrowers being encouraged to overstate their income and borrow more than they can afford;

◆ lending accentuates social inequalities – perceived high-risk borrowers are charged higher rates of interest, trapping them with higher burdens of debt and in extreme circumstances, over-indebtedness can lead to depression and suicide;

◆ lending accentuates business cycles – business downturns can become more disastrous on account of lending activity or inactivity.

Lending has been found to be **procyclical**, that is, there is a condition of positive correlation between lending and the overall state of the economy. It has been observed that lending often increases significantly during business cycle expansions and then falls considerably during subsequent downturns, sometimes leading to a severe shortfall in liquidity described as a 'credit crunch'. These changes in lending are generally more than proportional to the changes in economic activity, suggesting that bank loan supply tends to accentuate the business cycle. Provision for bad debts and write-offs start making their appearance towards the end of a period of expansion, and rise significantly during the downturn that follows, suggesting that lenders may take more risks during the expansion, but that it takes some time for the impact of these risks to be felt (Berger and Udell, 2004). This procyclicality is observed to be more marked in private banks than it is in state-owned banks; hence the latter are more likely to play a credit smoothing role in developing economies, while the former are more likely to accentuate business cycles in developed economies (Micco and Panizza, 2006).

During his tenure as the US Federal Reserve Chairman, Alan Greenspan (2001) observed that 'the worst loans are made at the top of the business cycle'; he also observed that at the bottom of the cycle, 'the problem is not making bad loans . . . it is not making any loans, whether good or bad, to credit-worthy customers', which is consistent with the significant fall in lending noted during cyclical downturns and as it is happening at the time of writing (early 2008) from the latter half of 2007.

During boom times, both lenders and borrowers tend to make unrealistic assumptions that growth will continue forever. Psychologists have considered 'herd instinct' to be a powerful force motivating human behaviour and there is growing evidence of herd behaviour in financial markets. Herd behaviour can emerge when aggressive lenders are valued by existing and potential employers and, as a result, even more cautious lenders are forced to become less conservative. Such competition-induced herd behaviour is liable to lead to periods during which lenders drive each other into strong credit expansions which are succeeded by periods during which lenders are slowed down by losses from earlier lending. Thus herd behaviour introduces cyclical behaviour into the aggregate supply of credit, giving rise to inefficient credit cycles in the economy (Devenow and Welch, 1996; Röthelia, 2001).

10.2   Responsible lending

To act responsibly is to act in a reliable and trustworthy manner, recognising a moral duty and accountability even in circumstances under which there are no specific legal obligations; it implies assuming a duty to individuals and to society as a whole.

Responsible lending covers a range of issues and practices.

'Responsible lending is more than just meeting the minimum legal requirements. It is also about driving forward best practice and treating customers fairly'. (Treasury, 2003)

Responsible lending involves the careful assessment of loan affordability.

The requirements for responsible lending (according to the FSA, 2003) are that the lender should:

◆ take account of the consumer's ability to repay;

◆ keep adequate records to show that they have taken account of the consumer's ability to repay;

◆ in the absence of evidence to the contrary, assume that repayments will be met from the consumer's main income.

Encouraging people to borrow what they want rather than what they can afford promotes an impression that borrowing is a glamorous and costless activity. Irresponsible lending in the form of opaque pricing structures and misleading marketing methods could lead to a situation of over-indebtedness. While there is no general agreement on what constitutes over-indebtedness, fears about **overindebtedness** have been on the rise in recent years. A Department of Trade and Industry (DTI) Task Force on Overindebtedness was set up in October 2000 to address concerns about consumer debt in the UK by considering ways of achieving more responsible lending and borrowing. The Task Force suggested the following definitions for households that indicated a high risk of being in, or getting into, financial difficulty.

According to the DTI (2003a), **over-indebtedness** means:

◆ having four or more current credit commitments (7% of all households);

◆ spending more than 25% of gross income (excluding mortgages) on consumer credit (5% of all households);

◆ spending more than 50% of gross income (including mortgages) on consumer credit (6% of all households).

Lenders will need to bear these indicators in mind and recognise the dangers of over-indebtedness.

10.2.1 Lending practices that are inconsistent with responsible lending

Citizens Advice (2003) identified seven key practices of credit card marketing that did not appear to be consistent with responsible lending practices:

1. speed and ease of application;

2. prominence given to very high credit limits;

3. prominence given to very low interest rates for cards where the interest rate paid by the consumer is determined by risk;

4. inducements to use the card;

5. unsolicited mailshots for credit card cheques;

6. important information in small print;

7. indiscriminate targeting of direct mailshots.

Some lending practices that have been recognised as inconsistent with responsible lending are as follows.

◆ A lack of transparency in charging systems, giving rise to difficulty experienced by consumers in deciding on best value. Such a lack of transparency in pricing obstructs effective competition and against consumers' interests. Complex charging structures mean that understanding interest rate calculations requires 'an unreasonable time and effort'. Different interest calculation methods (eg in the date from which interest starts) can cause wide differences in the amount actually charged. Lack of transparency of the lending process means that the loan terms and conditions are not always clear.

◆ Non-disclosure of fees, commission, inducements and other relevant information.

◆ Excessive charges.

◆ Inappropriate advice.

◆ Unsolicited communications or cold calling.

◆ Incentivising sales of particular products by payment of inducements.

◆ High-pressure selling.

◆ Automatic raising of credit limits without carrying out internal and external credit checks and without considering existing levels of indebtedness.

◆ Reducing repayment instalments to unviable levels.

◆ Inadequate credit checking.

◆ Excessive loan to value (LTV) ratios.

There is some evidence to show that the most successful loan recovery takes place when the loan-to-value ratio is below 66%, a condition that would have disqualified most of the recent sub-prime borrowers (Buttonwood, 2007).

◆ Recovery is generally costly and time-consuming. The average time taken is estimated to be 18 months, costing approximately 20–25% of the loan balance (Buttonwood, 2007).

◆ Re-ageing – loans are renewed at increased levels to cover delinquent interest, in order to report them as current rather than delinquent.

◆ Loan modification or restructuring, eg reducing the repayments or extending the loan repayment period.

Lenders modify loan terms and facilitate borrowers to make a few payments, enabling the classification of such loans as 'good' rather than 'bad'. The true level of credit exposure is masked by the inclusion of such loans into the pool of performing loans, distorting credit ratios and resulting in the skewed reporting of bad debts. Research suggests that modified loans suffer a 35–40% default rate over the following two years. (Buttonwood, 2007.)

◆ Predatory lending or lending to borrowers who cannot afford the repayments.

'There are currently no industry standards for modification and financial reporting, and no consumer safeguards to monitor or prohibit predatory practices'. (Mason, 2007.)

◆ Poor communication. The traditional banker, who had cast a kindly eye on the difficulties faced by a borrower, and was ready to listen to borrowers and rearrange loan terms if plausible reasons were adduced for delay in loan repayments, was perceived as a socially responsible individual. The modern lender, on the other hand, is perceived as distant and unsympathetic. Recent surveys indicate that, despite technological advances, lenders are still communicating with most borrowers by letter rather than adopting a more personal approach.

10.2.2 Corporate Social Responsibility (CSR)

Responsible lending is part of **Corporate Social Responsibility (CSR)**, whereby a business takes account of the economic, social and environmental impacts of its operations, maximising the benefits and minimising the downsides. CSR can be seen 'as the voluntary actions that business can take, over and above compliance with minimum legal requirements, to address both its own competitive interests and the interests of wider society' (DTI, 2003b).

Corporate social responsibility contributes to competitive advantage by:

◆ enhancing the capacity to innovate;

◆ enhancing corporate reputation, which is a driver of customer satisfaction;

◆ enhancing internal and external relationships;

◆ facilitating access to strategic assets such as licences to operate.

10.2.3 The importance of responsible lending

Responsible lending is important not only from the point of view of the consumer, but also from that of the lender. From the lender's point of view, responsible lending can lead to significant benefits.

◆ The perception of lenders as 'predators' and borrowers as 'struggling' does not do any good to the image of the lender. Responsible lending can promote the image of the lender as someone who can be trusted.

◆ A better image can lead to a better competitive position: a lender who is perceived to be responsible is seen to have a competitive advantage over others that are not.

◆ It is in the lender's own interest to recover money lent; responsible lending can result in better loan performance and recovery.

Thus responsible lending will constitute a superior business model from which both lenders and borrowers can benefit in the long term. As observed by Ellithorn (2007):'Banks should have a business model that is clear to consumers ... Relying on small print is not, in our view, a sustainable business model'.

10.3 Relationship lending and responsible lending

Lending can be transactional or based on an ongoing relationship. Responsible lending can be more evident when the lending is relational.

10.3.1 Transactional lending

A **transaction** consists of a trade of values between two parties: in this case, the lender and the borrower. The following are some of the characteristics of **transactional lending**:

◆ an arm's-length contract;

◆ strict adherence to contractual terms;

◆ many lenders competing for the consumer's business and the consumer shopping around with several lenders;

◆ a limited number of products;

◆ little in the way of a relationship existing between the two parties;

◆ information flows being significantly curtailed;

◆ a reduced scope for flexibility;

◆ is more evident in the USA and in the UK.

10.3.2 Relationship lending

Relationship lending is the process of creating, maintaining, and enhancing strong, value-laden relationships with customers. The following are some of the characteristics of relationship lending:

◆ a relational contract;

◆ undertaken over an extended period of time;

- the customer using a broad range of lending services;

- loan rates being usually established nominally at a spread above the base cost of funds;

- the focus of concern being the yield on the total activities;

- improved information flows between the parties;

- allows for flexibility of response;

- relationship lending is most evident in countries such as Japan and Germany, where there are cross-shareholdings between banks and non-financial corporations.

A relationship lending strategy will involve multiple interactions and multiple lending products. A relationship lender will have an informational advantage over a non-relationship lender and therefore a relationship lending strategy is more likely to generate future lending opportunities (Bharath et al, 2007). Relationship lending is likely to lead to responsible lending, because the lender has more to lose by irresponsible lending.

Conclusion

Lending is an activity that has existed from time immemorial and it will be an activity that will continue into the foreseeable future. Over the centuries, lending has taken on many shapes, from pawnbroking, to cheque cashing, to business lending, to credit derivatives. Lenders have alternatively taken on the hues of unscrupulous villains and benign saviours.

It is important that lenders should lend responsibly, because responsible lending provides the lender with ethical, as well as competitive, advantages. It is also important that lenders should lend cautiously and monitor meticulously, so that responsible consumers and shareholders and taxpayers do not have to pay too much to cover the consequences of irresponsible borrowing. Laws and codes have evolved over time to prevent irresponsible lending and to promote consumer protection. While laws were designed to protect unsophisticated borrowers from being exploited by unscrupulous moneylenders, they are capable of being used by unscrupulous borrowers to avoid paying their just debts to moneylenders (*Orakpo v Manson Investments Ltd* [1978]). To lend justly and to ensure that just debts are repaid – this is the challenge with which lenders will need to engage in times to come.

Further reading

Mason, J. R. (2007) 'Mortgage loan modification: promises and pitfalls', available online at www.criterioneconomics.com.

Topic 10

Review questions, activities and case study

The following review questions, activities and case study are designed to increase your understanding of the material you have just studied.

◆ The **review questions** are designed so that you can check your understanding of this topic.

◆ Completion of the **activities** will give you further opportunity to research and understand, in more depth, the themes running through this topic.

◆ The **case study** encourages you to think further about the application of the content of this topic.

The answers to the questions and case study are provided at the end of these learning materials. Please note that the activities are open-ended and therefore a suitable 'answer' may not always be provided.

Review questions

?

1. Identify some of the economic and social effects of lending.

2. What do you understand by 'responsible lending'?

3. What might be the criteria for overindebtedness? How might lenders be contributing to the problem?

4. Identify some of the lending practices that might be described as inconsistent with responsible lending.

5. Why is it important to lend responsibly?

Activity

Activity 1

Visit the following websites and search for 'Corporate Social Responsibility':

http://www.csr.gov.uk

http://www.citizensadvice.org.uk/

http://www.fsa.gov.uk

Activity 2

Read the summary of the House of Commons, Session 2003-04, Select Committee on Treasury – First Report on 'The Transparency of Credit Card Charges' as available at http://www.publications.parliament.uk/pa/cm200304/cmselect/cmtreasy/125/12503.htm.

Identify issues that you think are inconsistent with responsible lending.

Case study – Britain's streets of debt

Marion McDonald found the body of her husband Mark on a railway line in January 2005. There was no suicide note, but his backpack was filled with bank statements revealing massive indebtedness. He seemed to have killed himself because his debt went out of control.

Jeannette Sharratt borrowed £2,500 at extortionate interest rates, because of which the debt increased to over £100,000. The lender wanted her house and she lived under the threat of repossession for 16 years. Ultimately, the court ruled in favour of the borrower.

> Gwen Colbourne was 72 years old and lived on a small pension, but had three store cards, six credit cards two loans and no assets.
>
> *Source:* BBC One, 5–9 June 2006

1   What is 'responsible lending'?

2   Identify any evidence of irresponsible lending in relation to the problems faced by the borrowers above.

3   What might be the impact of irresponsible lending decisions?

4   What do lenders need to do in order to meet the FSA requirements for responsible lending?

5   What is the lesson here for lenders?

Appendix A
Answers to review questions

Topic 1   Introduction to lending principles

1.   See section 1.3.2.

2.   See section 1.3.2.

3.   See section 1.3.3.

4.   See section 1.4.

5.   See section 1.5.1.

Case study – turmoil in the credit markets – 2007

1   Sub-prime lending, or lending to individuals who will be unable to meet their debt obligations.

2   Sub-prime lending is lending to individuals who are not considered to be prime or good borrowers.

3   Northern Rock's strategy of short-term borrowing and long-term lending was highly profitable under conditions of credit boom. When funds ran dry, the bank was pushed to the brink of insolvency. Profitability had run counter to liquidity requirements.

4   Borrowers can default; banks can accumulate bad debt and be pushed to the brink of insolvency; the entire financial system can experience a severe shortage of cash and loss of confidence.

5   Lenders need toevaluate carefully the quality of the borrower and their ability to meet interest payments prior to making any loans. Lenders need to perform a careful balancing act of meeting the conflicting needs of profitability, liquidity and safety.

Topic 2   The legal and regulatory environment

1. See section 2.1.

2. See section 2.1.

3. See section 2.2.1.

4. See section 2.3.

5. See section 2.5.1.

Topic 3   Types of borrower

1. See the introduction to Topic 3.

2. See section 3.1.3.

3. See section 3.2.

4. See section 3.3.2.

5. See section 3.4.2.

Topic 4   The purposes of financing

1. ◆ See section 4.1.1.

    ◆ See section 4.1.3.

2. See section 4.2.3.

3. See section 4.2.4.

Case study

1 LA Gear failed to predict the change in fashion trends and adapt its products to suit changing customer needs.

2 It is important that a lender has a good knowledge of the industry and competition within which the borrower operates in order to be able to assess the asset quality. LA Gear, for example, collapsed and gave rise to losses for lenders despite strict loan covenants because the company as well as lenders failed to gauge the developments within the industry.

3 The company was able to fund operating losses by sale of marketable assets. By managing its working capital and selling excess inventories it kept going for a number of years. Despite strict loan covenants and large losses, the company was able to survive for a considerable length of time due largely to the liquidity of its asset base.

4 A high degree of asset liquidity, particularly the ability to liquidate working capital, might enable a company to survive financial difficulties for a considerable length of time.

Topic 5   Forms of lending

1. See section 5.2.1 and section 5.3.1.

2. See section 5.5.

3. See section 5.8.1.

4. See section 5.8.2.

Case study

1   Section 75 of the Consumer Credit Act 1974 establishes the principle of 'connected lender liability', whereby credit card issuers are liable for payments for products and services worth between £100 and £30,000, individually and jointly with suppliers, if a consumer has a valid claim against the supplier for misrepresentation or breach of contract relating to goods or services bought with a credit card.

2   A valid claim will need to involve misrepresentation or breach of contract relating to goods or services bought with a credit card.

3   No. It was found that no misrepresentation was involved.

4   A lender who has provided a credit card to a UK borrower will be liable along with the supplier, if the borrower used the card abroad to pay for goods and services that are deemed to be defective or misrepresented.

Topic 6   The lending cycle – the credit granting process

1. See section 6.1.

2. See section 6.2.5.

3. See section 6.3.4.1 and section 6.3.4.2.

4. See section 6.5.1.

Activities

Activity 1

Working capital ratio (CA – CL)	-3,802	-3,063	-2,783
Current ratio (CA ÷ CL)	0.60	0.68	0.77

The working capital ratio is negative and the ratio has been declining over the past three years. This will require further investigation and analysis, as well as a comparison with other companies in the same industry.

Case study

1 The loan agreement and facility letter.

2 The loan agreement stated that the overdraft was payable on demand, while the facility letter indicated that the overdraft was provided for a period of 12 months.

3 Overdrafts are generally considered to have the attribute of being repayable on demand, but an express clause in a loan document can override this attribute.

4 The overdraft granted in *Titford* was held to be not repayable on demand because the facility letter stated that the overdraft was provided for a period of 12 months.

5 Lenders need to pay particular attention to the clauses in loan documents and to ensure that there are no contradictions that might vitiate their claim for repayment.

Topic 7   Security – general

1. See section 7.5.1.

2. See section 7.1.

3. See section 7.4.

4. See section 7.3.

5. See section 7.5.2.

Case study – *West Bromwich Building Society v Wilkinson* [2005]

1 The security obtained by West Bromwich Building Society was the house in Norfolk, which was purchased Mark and Lynne Wilkinson in October 1988.

2 Possible reasons for the shortfall in the sale proceeds of the collateral security might be: the decline in the property market at that time, poor condition or location of the property as indicated by the time taken to negotiate a sale, and the forced sale risk of loss in asset value.

3 The Limitation Act 1980 is so named because it provides time limits within which action may be taken for breaches of the law.

4 12 years.

5 More than 12 years had elapsed after the loan became repayable in 1989 before the legal action that was commenced by the building society in 2002.

6 Lenders need to monitor loan accounts carefully and take prompt remedial action to ensure that their claim is not invalidated by the operation of the Limitation Act 1980. Lenders need to recognise that obtaining collateral security does not necessarily preclude them from incurring loan losses.

Topic 8   Security – specific forms

1. See the introduction to Topic 8.

2. ◆ See section 8.1.2 and section 8.1.3.

   ◆ See section 8.2.4 and section 8.2.5.

   ◆ See section 8.3.2 and section 8.3.3.

   ◆ See section 8.3.2 and section 8.4.4.

3. See section 8.5.2 and section 8.5.3.

4. See section 8.6.2.

5. See section 8.6.2.

Case study – *Barclays Bank plc v O'Brien* [1994]

1 The security obtained by Barclays Bank for the business loan given to Mr O'Brien's company was the guarantee of Mr O'Brien secured by a legal charge signed by Mr and Mrs O'Brien on their matrimonial home situated at Farnham Lane in Slough.

2 Mr O'Brien misrepresented to Mrs O'Brien that the charge was to secure only £60,000 and that even this liability would be released in a short time when the house was remortgaged. In reality, the current level of the facilities granted to the company amounted to £107,000 and this was projected to increase to £135,000.

3 No. It was found that, in such cases, there was no need for any special treatment to wives if the doctrine of notice was properly applied.

4 The lender had constructive notice of the wrongful misrepresentation made by Mr O'Brien to Mrs O'Brien, but had failed to take 'reasonable steps' to make Mrs O'Brien 'fully aware of the nature of the documentation to be signed'. Burnham branch of Barclays Bank did not give Mrs O'Brien any explanation of the effect of the documents. No one suggested that she should take independent legal advice. She did not read the documents or the accompanying side letter. She was not even given a copy of the guarantee.

5 There are a number of lessons here for lenders.

   ◆ A lender needs to be aware of the circumstances in which guarantees are signed and to take reasonable steps as required by the law in order to ensure that obligations are not avoided by guarantors on account of undue influence.

   ◆ The availability of security should not cloud the lender's ability to judge the viability of a business proposition.

   ◆ Security is only a fallback arrangement and should not be deemed to be the primary source of repayment.

Topic 9   The lending cycle – the monitoring and control process

1. See section 9.1.

2. See section 9.2.

3. See section 9.3.1.

4. See section 9.3.3.

Topic 10 The impact of lending and social responsibility

1. See section 10.1.

2. See section 10.2.

3. See section 10.2.

4. See section 10.2.1.

5. See section 10.2.3.

Case study – Britain's streets of debt

1 For a discussion on responsible lending see section 10.2.

2 Irresponsible lending evident in relation to the problems faced by the borrowers includes:

   ◆ lending without regard to the consumer's ability to repay;

   ◆ extortionate rates of interest;

   ◆ not assuming that repayments will be met from the consumer's main income in the absence of evidence to the contrary.

3 Irresponsible lending decisions can lead to:

   ◆ the loss of consumer lives;

   ◆ the loss of income for the lender in the form of lost income and legal costs;

   ◆ the poor image for the lender.

4 Lenders need to:

   ◆ take account of the consumer's ability to repay;

   ◆ keep adequate records to show that they have taken account of the consumer's ability to repay;

   ◆ in the absence of evidence to the contrary, assume that repayments will be met from the consumer's main income.

5 It is important that lenders should lend responsibly, because responsible lending provides the lender with ethical, as well as competitive, advantages.

Index

178